Contents

Part Three: Stars and Space

Activities in this section are intended to help students understand the three-dimensional space that exists beyond the boundaries of our solar system.

Part 1

The Earth and the Moon

Background

Earth is the third of nine planets that orbit the sun, an average-sized star on the outer edge of the Milky Way Galaxy. Out of all the planets, Earth is the only one with liquid water on its surface and the only one with life as we know it.

Planet Earth is not a true sphere. Its circumference measured at the equator is about 45 km greater than its circumference measured around the poles. It orbits the sun in a slightly elliptical path, causing its distance from the sun to vary from 145 million km at its closest approach in early January to 152 million km in early July.

Earth has one natural satellite orbiting it. Although its official name is "Luna," the rocky satellite is more commonly known as "the moon." The moon orbits the Earth once every 29.5 days, which is also the period of one Earth month. Because of this phenomenon, the same side of the moon always faces the Earth.

Although the moon's gravitational pull (about a sixth of Earth's) is strong enough to affect the tides on Earth, it is too weak to hold down an atmosphere. Because it has no atmosphere to modify its climate, the moon's surface temperature ranges from 120 degrees Celsius (water boils at 100 degrees Celsius) during its day to - 180 degrees during its night.

According to information gathered by geologists, both the Earth and the moon are about 4.6 billion years old. That places their formation at about the same time as the rest of the solar system.

With all of these numbers, probably the best place to begin an exploration of math in space is right at home. The Earth and the moon present countless opportunities for computation, measurement, and problem solving, and the activities in this section will help to get you started.

Note: Reproduce pages 5 and 6 for students doing this activity.

Hands Around the Earth

This is a cooperative activity for groups of four. Its purpose is to demonstrate how large the Earth is in a way that students can easily understand. Students are asked to create a proposal for an event called "Hands Around the World." During the event, people from all over the world will hold hands in a line that stretches around the Earth on the equator or along a line of longitude.

Working together, students will plan the route of the event and determine how many people must be recruited to make the event a success. While doing that, students will read and interpret data, measure in meters and centimeters, estimate, compute, and make group decisions.

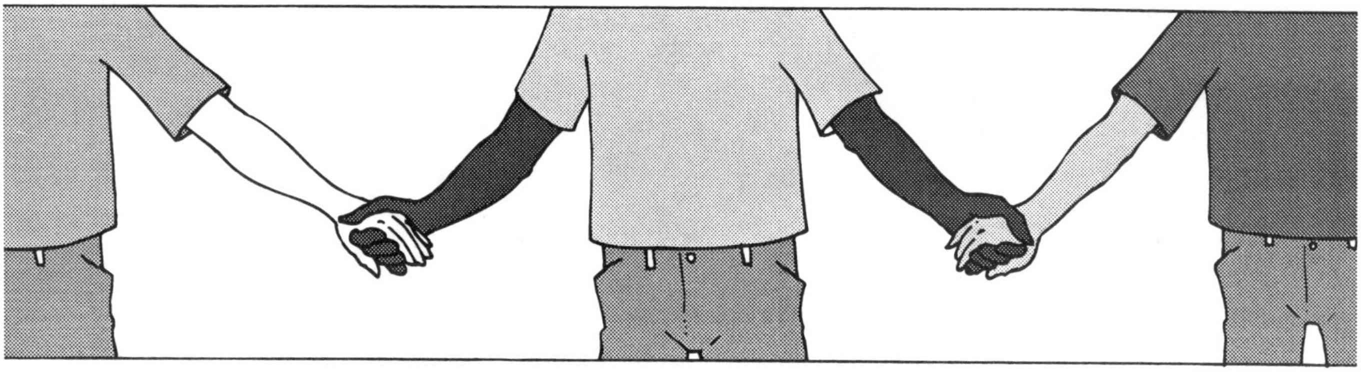

Hints, Tips, and Suggestions

Begin by selecting groups of four and assigning a role to each student in the group. A description of the roles is found on page 6. Precut the role cards and fill in the names of the group members. Cut out the facts card and the problems card and attach them to the appropriate role cards. Begin by asking each Data Analyst to read the telegram to his or her group. Discuss the event with your students, then ask them to work together to solve their problems.

Several classroom globes should be available for groups to use when they are solving their first problem - selecting a route for the activity.

Extending the Activity

- Create posters and press releases to advertise the event or to recruit volunteers.
- Invent individual flotation devices and insulating clothing for participants who will be on lakes, rivers, or oceans or who will be crossing the poles.
- Calculate how many hot dogs (10 to a package), buns (8 to a package), and bags of chips (4 servings to a bag) will be needed to provide lunch to all the participants. Calculate how much lunch will cost, based on local food prices.
- Pretend that at the end of the event each participant shook hands with all the other participants. Find some way to calculate how many handshakes were exchanged. (The formula for finding the number of handshakes is N x (N - 1) / 2, where N = the number of participants.)
- Create a 10 centimeter diameter medallion to commemorate the event.

URGENT TELEGRAM URGENT TELEGRAM URGENT

28-03470-3393- 23151795
TO: SCIENCE PROBLEM-SOLVING TEAM
FROM: DEPARTMENT OF SCIENCE CHALLENGES
SUBJECT: PROJECT HANDS AROUND THE WORLD

A FEW YEARS AGO, A GROUP OF PEOPLE ORGANIZED AN ACTIVITY CALLED **HANDS ACROSS AMERICA**. THEIR OBJECTIVE WAS TO LINE UP ENOUGH PEOPLE STANDING SIDE BY SIDE HOLDING HANDS TO REACH ACROSS THE UNITED STATES FROM THE ATLANTIC OCEAN TO THE PACIFIC OCEAN. ALTHOUGH THE PROJECT WAS NOT ENTIRELY SUCCESSFUL, MILLIONS OF PEOPLE JOINED ENOUGH HANDS TO STRETCH ACROSS SMALL TOWNS AND LARGE CITIES, OVER MOUNTAINS, AND ACROSS MILES OF FARM FIELDS.

THE SAME PROMOTERS ARE PLANNING A NEW ACTIVITY CALLED **HANDS AROUND THE WORLD**. THIS TIME THEY WOULD LIKE TO LINE UP ENOUGH PEOPLE TO REACH ENTIRELY AROUND THE EARTH EITHER ON A LINE OF LONGITUDE OR ON THE EQUATOR. THEY NEED ASSISTANCE WITH THEIR PROJECT AND I HAVE SUGGESTED THAT YOUR GROUP HELP THEM.

THE PROJECT DIRECTOR IN YOUR GROUP HAS MORE INFORMATION ABOUT THE PROBLEMS WHICH NEED TO BE SOLVED. I AM DEPENDING UPON YOUR GROUP TO ARRIVE AT A PRACTICAL SOLUTION AND BE ABLE TO DESCRIBE IT TO THE PROMOTERS.

URGENT TELEGRAM URGENT TELEGRAM URGENT

FOR THE PROJECT DIRECTOR ONLY

Your group has two problems to solve. When you are done, the Quality Control member of your group should be able to describe the answers to these problems and tell how your group solved them.

Problem #1
Decide upon the best route to follow - either along a line of longitude or along the equator. (Although the promoters have devised a way to keep people warm in arctic weather and can support them over large stretches of water, they prefer crossing as much land as possible.)

Problem #2
Calculate how many people will be needed to successfully complete the task of ringing the globe. (You may need to devise an experiment to get the information you will need to solve this problem.)

FOR THE DATA ANALYST ONLY

Earth Facts:

Diameter - 12,756 km
Period of rotation - 23 hours 54 minutes
Period of revolution - 365.25 days
Average temperature - 15 degrees Celsius
Number of moons: One
Distance from Sun - 155,000,000 km
Density (water = 1) - 5.51

Measurement Facts:

10 millimeters = one centimeter
100 cm = 1 meter
100 meters = one kilometer
1000 grams = one kilogram

NAME

PROJECT DIRECTOR

Read the information on the **For The Project Director Only** card to your group, and make sure that everyone in your group understands what needs to be done.

Decide how the group will go about solving the two problems, and direct your group in the activities.

NAME

MATERIALS MANAGER

Cut out and assemble the metric tape measure on this page.

Gather any other materials that the group needs to complete the tasks. Return the materials when your group is done with them.

NAME

DATA ANALYST

Your job is to read the telegram to the members of your group and make sure they understand it.

You are also in charge of the Earth Facts card. Nobody else in your group may hold or look at the card. It is up to you to provide the information that group members need as they ask for it.

NAME

QUALITY CONTROL SUPERVISOR

Make sure that each of the problems has been solved satisfactorily and that all the information that the group has collected is accurate.

Be ready to report your findings to the entire class in the form of an oral report along with a graph or chart.

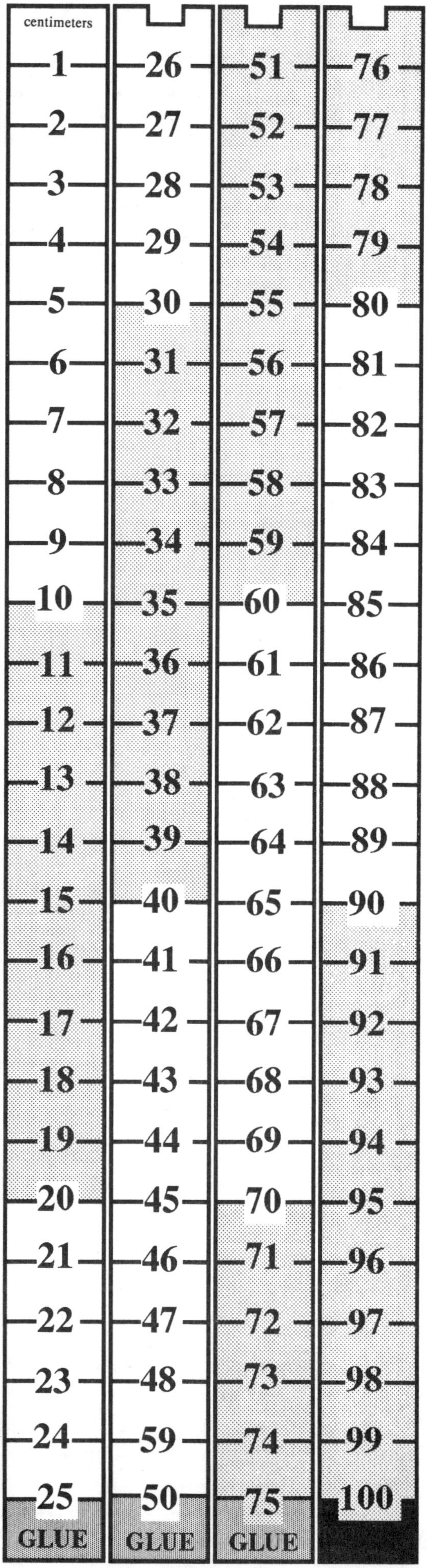

The Great Race

A Cooperative Activity for Groups of Two

Pretend that someone has invented a way to jog at a constant speed of 9.6 km per hour non-stop day and night over land and water, up mountains and down canyons, through jungles and across deserts. Also pretend that they are going to demonstrate their ability to do this by jogging non-stop around the Earth at the equator.

Work together with a partner to find out how long it will take them.

You will need the following materials:

- calculator
- classroom globe
- calendar

Predict the amount of time you think it would take to jog around the Earth.

Partner #1 ______________________ Prediction ______________________________

Partner #2 ______________________ Prediction ______________________________

Here are some Earth facts you may need to know:

Length of day: 24 hours

Length of year: 365 days (Leap Year = 366 days; an extra day is added to February)

Leap years are years that can be divided by 4 without a remainder.

Leap centuries are centuries that can be divided by 4 without a remainder.

Earth diameter: approximately 13,000 km

Earth circumference: approximately 40,000 km

The race will start at exactly midnight of December 31st of this year. Work with your partner to calculate exactly how long it should take for the runner to complete the entire race.

Pretend that news reporters would like to videotape the completion of the race. Since their time is limited, they will need to know the exact day and time the runner is expected to cross the finish line.

Use the information on this page to calculate the precise month, day, hour, and minute the runner can be expected to finish the race.

Note: Reproduce page 10 for students doing this activity.

The Force of Earth's Atmosphere

Like everything else on Earth, air is pulled downwards by gravity, giving it weight. You can prove that air has weight by measuring the mass of the same balloon inflated and deflated. The difference in mass is the weight of the air that was inside the balloon.

Air also has pressure, which is the force exerted on objects by the weight of the atmosphere. When astronauts travel into the vacuum of space, they take along with them their own supply of air pressure. Whether it is in their spacecraft or inside a spacesuit, air pressure is absolutely vital for their survival.

At sea level on an average day, air exerts a pressure of about 1.14 kilograms per square centimeter. That is approximately the weight of two boxes of butter pressing down on an area the size of your little fingernail. Ouch!

We really don't feel all that pressure because our bodies are equally squeezed from all sides and because our bodies, composed mostly of water, push back on the atmosphere with equal force. But we can sense air pressure whenever it changes - such as when we ascend in an elevator or an airplane.

Teacher Demonstration

This activity begins with a simple, but dramatic experiment that will show your students the crushing pressure of Earth's atmosphere.

Materials:

- a hot plate (and extension cord)
- a large container of cold water
- several empty soft drink cans
- a heat-proof mitt
- a wrench-type jar opener

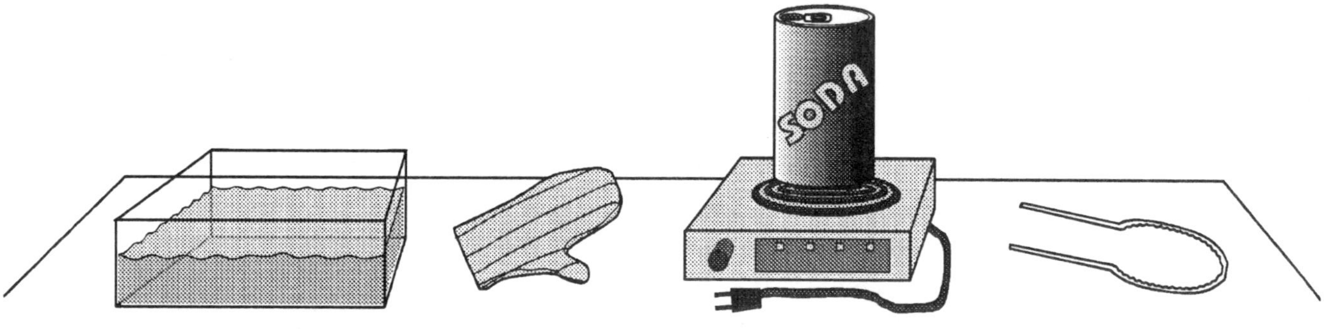

1. Pour about 45 ml of water into the can and heat it until it boils. Allow steam to escape from the can for a few minutes while you solicit from your students what they know about air pressure.

2. Wearing a hot mitt for protection, grasp the can around the middle with the jar opener. In one quick motion, remove the can from the heat and plunge it with the opening downwards into the container of water. Be ready for a dramatic surprise as atmospheric pressure crushes the can with a muffled "whomp."

How It Works:
Heat causes the liquid water in the can to change its state and become a high-temperature vapor called steam. As it does, the air which previously filled the can is pushed out and entirely replaced by the heavier steam.

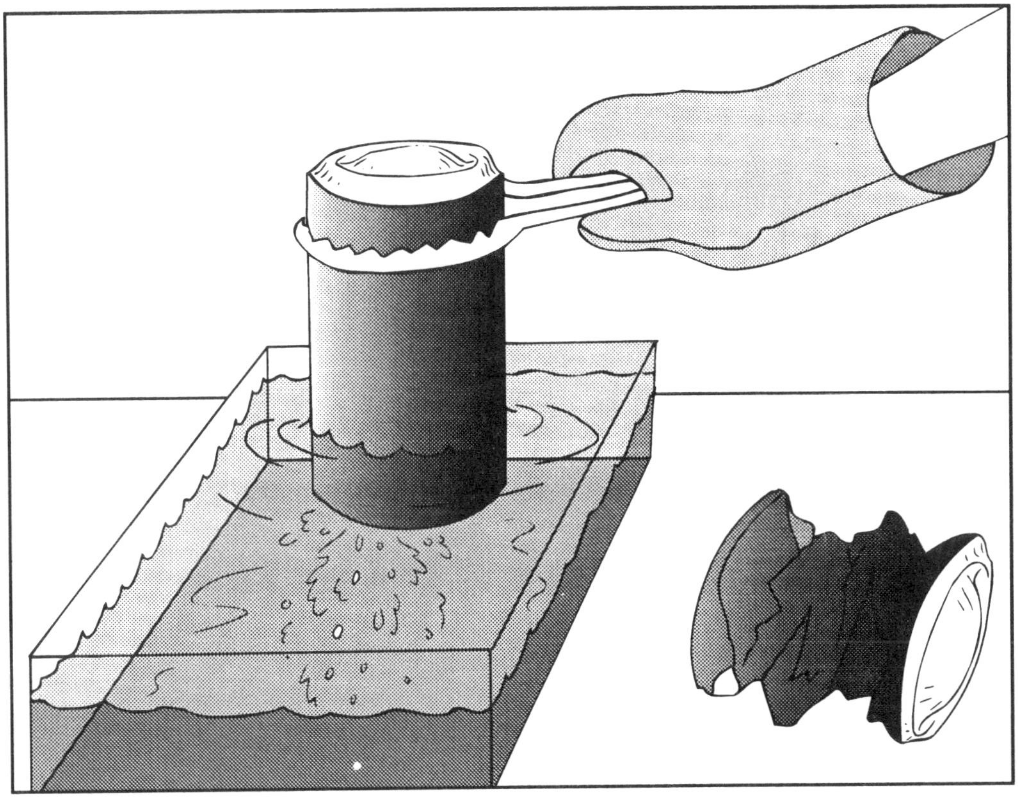

When the opening of the can is plunged into water, the vapor suddenly condenses back into liquid leaving a partial vacuum inside the can. As Aristotle theorized, nature abhors a vacuum and begins to find ways to fill it with outside atmosphere. At first water is pushed up into the can, but that can't happen fast enough to prevent air pressure from smashing in on the can from all sides, dramatically collapsing it.

About the Student Activity:
Ask your students to calculate the surface area of the can in order to compute how much air pressure was pushing in on the can at the instant it collapsed. Each group will need an empty soft drink can, a metric tape measure (page 47), and the activity sheet (page 10).

Ask them to work together using the formulas and information on the activity page to calculate the surface area of the can. Some students might be able to derive a formula for finding the surface area of any cylinder. For your benefit, the formula is: Area = $2(\Pi r^2) + (C \times H)$ where C is the circumference of the can and H is its height.

Have them multiply the area of the can by the atmospheric pressure at sea level, which is about 1.14 kilogram per square centimeter. If your students are accurate with their calculations, they will find that between three and four hundred kilograms of air pressure smashed the can.

Extending the Activity

- A suction cup is held to a wall or window by air pressure. The force needed to dislodge it is equal to the amount of air pressure holding it down. Calculate the surface area of the suction disk and determine the amount of pressure that is holding it, then pull against the disk with a kilogram spring scale. The suction cup should release at a pull equal to the air pressure pushing against it.
- Build a simple barometer to measure air pressure. Record the measurements for a week and compare them to changes in the weather.
- Find out how meteorologists use differences in air pressure to predict changes in the weather.

The Crushing Force of Earth's Atmosphere

Student Activity

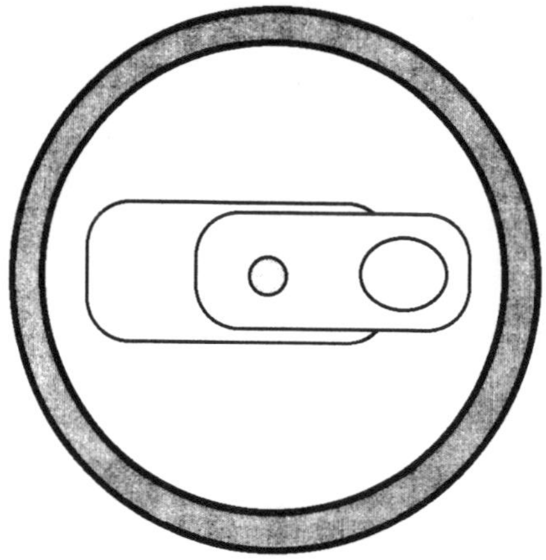

During the experiment performed by your teacher, a tremendous amount of air pressure pushed in on the soft drink can causing it to suddenly implode. Your task will be to calculate exactly how much pressure there was on the can.

Do the following to determine the amount of air pressure pushing against the can at the moment it collapsed:

1. Calculate the entire surface area of the can in square centimeters.

2. Multiply the surface area by 1.14 kilogram per square centimeter. The final answer is the total kilograms of air pressure pushing against the can.

On the bottom of the page is a metric ruler that you may want to clip out and use to measure your can.

On the right side of this page is a full-size drawing of the top and side of a soft drink can. Use it to keep track of the dimensions of the can and your final calculations.

Here are some mathematical formulas you may need:

Circumference of a circle = pi x diameter

Area of a rectangle = length x width

Area of a circle = pi x radius^2

pi = 3.14

radius = 1/2 diameter

Challenge:

Can you devise a single formula that can be used to calculate the surface area of any cylinder?

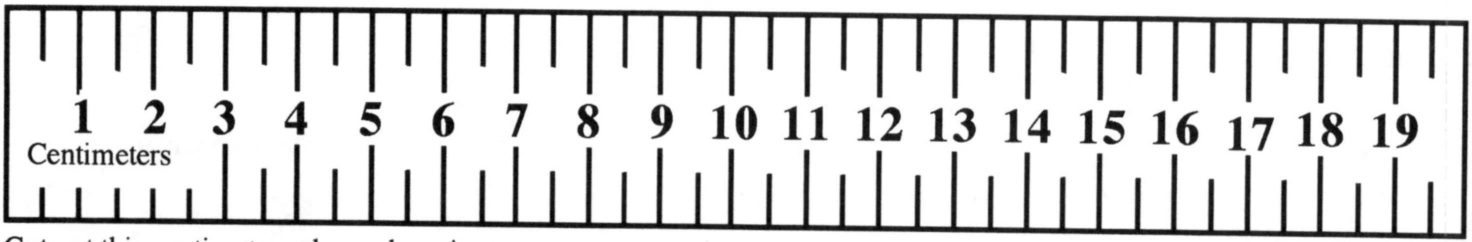

Cut out this centimeter ruler and use it to measure your soft drink can.

Note: Reproduce page 13 for students doing this activity.

Modeling the Earth and the Moon

Pencil ready? Here is a quick quiz.
1. Compared to the size of the Earth, how large is the moon? If the Earth was the size of a basketball, how large would the moon be? The size of a a softball? A ping-pong ball? A soccer ball?

2. How far away from the Earth is the moon? If the Earth were the size of a basketball and you held it in your left hand, would the scale distance to the moon fit within your outstretched arms? What do you think?

Don't feel badly if you are not sure about the answer to either of these questions. The drawings of the Earth and the moon in science textbooks try to show the comparative sizes of these objects and the distance between them, but nothing demonstrates it as well as scale models, and you can easily make them with any classroom globe.

To do these demonstrations for your students you will need the following materials:

- a classroom globe
- twelve meters of string
- scissors
- several different sports balls (Soccer, tennis, racquetball, ping-pong, softball, and baseball spheres will suffice.)

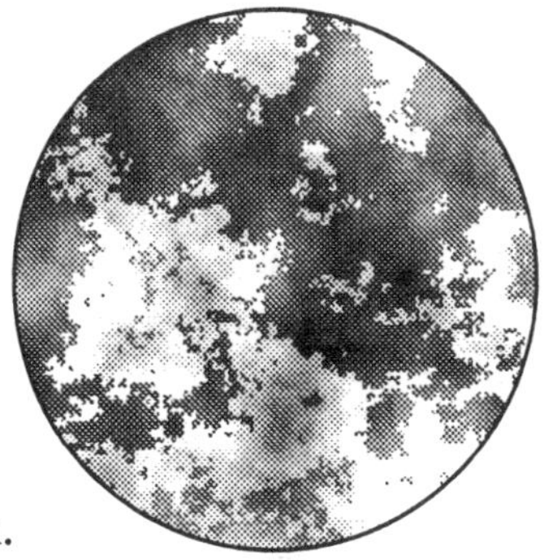

Earth

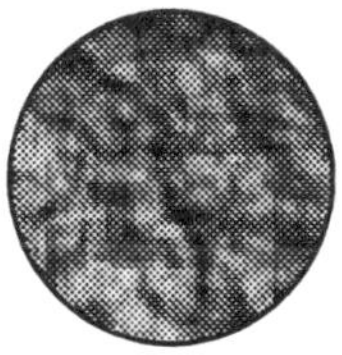

Moon

Teacher Demonstration: How Big is the Moon?

Before reading any further, make a prediction about which ball you think represents the scale size of the moon if the Earth was really the size of your classroom globe. Make sure you ask your students to make the same prediction before completing this demonstration for them.

Here are some Earth and moon facts you will need to know: The diameter of the moon is approximately 3,150 km. That is about one fourth the diameter of Earth. (Does that mean the circumference of the moon is also one fourth that of the Earth? This is a good question to ask your upper grade students. The answer is yes.)

Directions:

1. Wrap string once around the equator of your classroom globe. Cut the string to that length.
2. Quarter the length of the string by folding it in half twice. (Ask your students how many other ways they can think of to quarter the length of the string.)
3. Find a sports ball whose circumference closely matches the length of the quartered string. For the average classroom globe, a baseball or softball is a good starting place. (Once you've found the correct sphere, you might want to ask your students how many ways they can think of to prove it is the correct one).

Is your discovery surprising? How closely did it match your prediction?

Teacher Demonstration: How Far Away is the Moon?

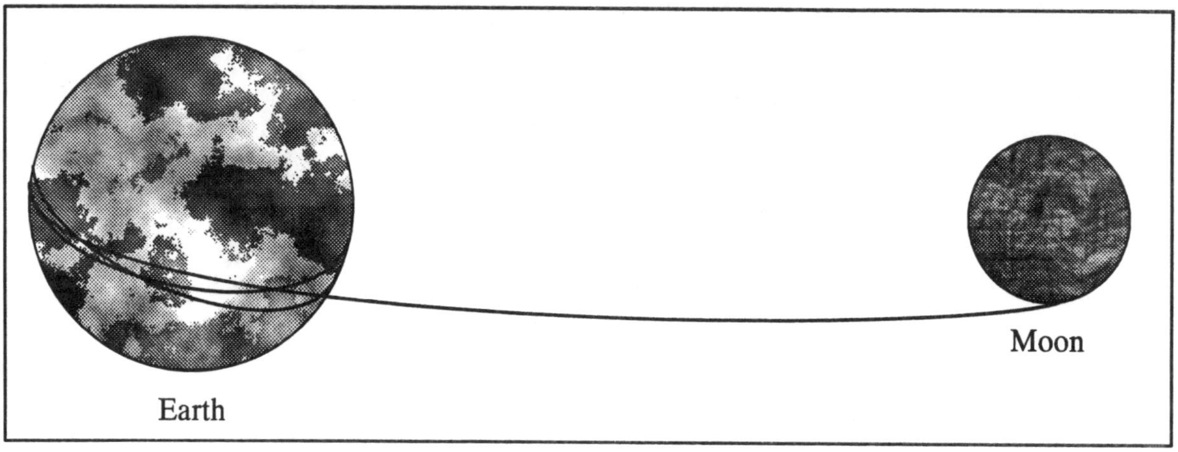

Before reading further, stop and make a prediction. Put the globe on a desk or table and move away from it until you think you are at the correct scale distance that the moon is away from the Earth. Mark your spot. Have your students make the same kind of a physical prediction before showing them this demonstration.

Here are more Earth and moon facts you will need to know: The approximate circumference of the earth is 40,000 kilometers. The approximate distance between the Earth and the moon is 400,000 kilometers. By placing the smaller number above the larger, you create a 1 to 10 ratio. That means that the moon is ten times the circumference of the Earth away from the Earth.

Directions:

1. Wrap the string once around the equator of your globe. Mark that length off along the edge of a table. Keep measuring out more string until its total length is ten times Earth's circumference. Cut the string and wrap it around a tube or bottle to keep it from tangling.

2. Hold the roll of string near the globe. Have a student hold the free end of the string against the moon ball and walk the moon away from the the globe until the string is completely unwound. (You may need to do this in a hallway or in a multi-purpose room.)

The stretched-out string demonstrates the actual scale distance from the Earth to the moon. How closely did it match your prediction? Are you surprised? Why? How closely does it match the drawings in your science book?

Extending the Activity

Use the information gained from "The Great Race" activity to calculate how many days (or years) it would take to jog to the moon. Answer: About 4.7 years.

If you could drive a car to the moon at a constant speed of 100 kilometers per hour, how long would it take to get there? Answer: About 4,000 hours or 166 days. Pack a big lunch.

When astronauts visited the moon, they left behind laser reflectors used to measure the distance between the Earth and the moon. Traveling at the speed of light, how long would it take for laser light to make the round trip from Earth to the reflector and back to Earth?

Modeling the Earth and Moon
Student Activity

You can make a scale model of the Earth and moon and show their scale distance apart--and it will all fit on your desktop. To do it, you will need the following materials:

- modeling clay
- calculator
- mini-micrometer
- metric tape measure

(Metric measurement tools are on page 47. Assemble the metric measurement tools according to the directions on the page.)

All the data you will need is in this box.
Diameter of Earth: 13,000 km
Circumference of Earth: 40,000 km
Diameter of moon: 3,250 km
Circumference of moon: 10,000 km
Average distance between the Earth and the moon: 400,000 km
Diameter of the sun: 1,392,000 km
Average distance between the sun and the Earth: 150,000,000 km

The scale size for this activity is:
1 centimeter = 6,500 kilometers
That is the same as saying the width of your little finger is equal to the distance from San Francisco to Tokyo.

Directions:

1. To make a scale model of the Earth, divide its diameter by 6,500. The answer will be in centimeters and millimeters (there are ten millimeters in one centimeter). Roll a clay sphere equal to the scale diameter and put it aside.

2. Make a scale model of the moon by dividing its diameter by 6,500. Roll a clay sphere equal to its scale diameter and put it aside.

3. Calculate the scale distance between the Earth and the moon by dividing the actual distance by 6,500.

4. Place the sphere representing the Earth on one corner of your desk. Measure towards the opposite corner and place the moon sphere at its scale distance from the Earth.

Challenges:

- At this same scale, how large would a clay sphere have to be to represent the sun?
- At this same scale, how many centimeters away would the sun be? How many meters is that? (There are 100 centimeters in one meter.)
- The average distance between the Earth and the moon is 400,000 km. Research to find the closest distance and the farthest distance they are apart and model them in this same way.

Part 2

Our Sun and its Satellites

Background

Stars vary considerably in size. Large ones like Aldebaran in the constellation Taurus have diameters that are hundreds of times that of our sun. Small ones like the white dwarf star that orbits Sirius may be only thousands of kilometers in diameter but are so dense that a few milliliters of their star stuff would weigh several metric tons.

The largest known star, named IRS-5, has a diameter nearly 11,000 times that of our sun. The smallest known star, named LP327-186 because of its location on star maps, is only about 1,600 km in diameter. To put the sizes in perspective, if IRS-5 was reduced to a sphere the height of Mt. Everest, LP327-186 would be the size of a jawbreaker. At that same scale, our sun would be the size of a large beachball.

Not all stars are the same color. The differences are caused by the temperature of their nuclear reactions. As metal is heated, it first glows red, then orange, yellow, blue, and finally white. The temperatures of stars are rated according to the same kind of color shift with red stars being the coolest and white stars the hottest.

For example, Betelgeuse, the giant red star in the Orion constellation, is a relatively cool 2,200 degrees Celsius while Rigel, a giant blue star in the same constellation, has a temperature of about 25,000 degrees Celsius. Our sun is a yellow star with a temperature of about 10,000 degrees Celsius.

Most of the stars we see in the night sky are within the boundaries of our own Milky Way galaxy. Some stars are distinctive and easily recognized. But the majority of the billions of stars in the Milky Way are visible only through a powerful telescope. Those are the stars that make up the hazy ribbon that stretches across the sky on moonless nights.

Our sun is an average-sized star located about 3/4 of the way out from the center of the Milky Way. Although small compared to some other stars, our sun is unique. Of all the stars in the Milky Way, it is so far the only one that astronomers are absolutely positive has planets and other satellites orbiting it.

Please Line Up

This is a cooperative activity for groups of four. By sharing clues with each other, students will logically deduce the order of the planets.

Hints, Tips, and Suggestions

Select a member of the cooperative group to be the materials manager. Ask the materials manager to cut apart the clue cards and planet cards on page 16 before beginning the formal activity. Also ask your students to read and follow the directions on their clue card and to not show their clues to anyone. The students will know they are successful when the order of the planets matches all of the clues on their clue cards.

It is difficult for some students to memorize the order of the planets, so try teaching your students this linguistic tool. The order of the first letters of the planets is M V E M J S U N P. These can become the first letters of words that make a silly, but memorable sentence such as "My Very Elderly Mother Just Sewed Uncle Nate's Pajamas."

Extensions

Have your students create their own silly sentences from words that begin with this letter sequence.

Although many people think Pluto is the planet farthest from the sun, that is not always true. The orbit of Pluto lies in a different plane than the other planets. Its slightly inclined path actually takes Pluto inside the orbit of Neptune for part of its solar year. Research to find out when this occurs. (Right now is one of those times. Pluto is presently the eighth planet from the sun and won't resume its "normal" position as the ninth planet until 1999.)

Please Line Up

A Cooperative Activity for Groups of Four

Goal: To work together to place the planets of the solar system in their proper order based on their distance from the sun.

Directions: Cut out the planet cards. Cut out the clue cards and pass them out to the members of your group. Read the directions on the clue card. You will reach the goal when the order of the planets matches the clues on all the cards.

These are your clues. You may read your clues to other group members, but **you may not show them to anyone.**

- Uranus is between Neptune and Saturn.
- Jupiter is closer to Earth than Neptune is.

These are your clues. You may read your clues to other group members, but **you may not show them to anyone.**

- Venus is Earth's nearest neighbor.
- There are seven planets between Mercury and Pluto. Mercury is closest to the sun.

These are your clues. You may read your clues to other group members, but **you may not show them to anyone.**

- The four planets nearest the sun are smaller than the next four planets.
- Earth is third from the sun.
- Saturn is not eighth from the sun.

These are your clues. You may read your clues to other group members, but **you may not show them to anyone.**

- The fifth and sixth planets from the sun are larger than any of the others.
- Mars is not second from the sun.

Sun	Mercury	Uranus	Venus	Neptune	Saturn	Pluto	Earth	Jupiter	Mars

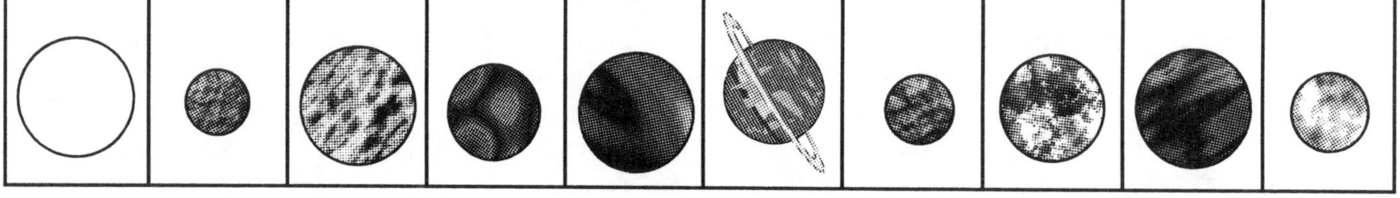

Note: Reproduce page 18 for students doing this activity.

Planet Profile Chart

Information about the sun and the planets is constantly changing. Astronomers and scientists are continually updating their records with new data that they obtain from observations and space probes. During this activity, students will research to find the most recent data regarding the sun and the planets of the solar system.

Hints and Tips

Have students work in groups of two to complete the chart. They should keep track of where they found their data and how recent their information is. Encourage your students to use as many sources of information as possible. (For your benefit, the Astrofacts on page 48 contain the most recent data.)

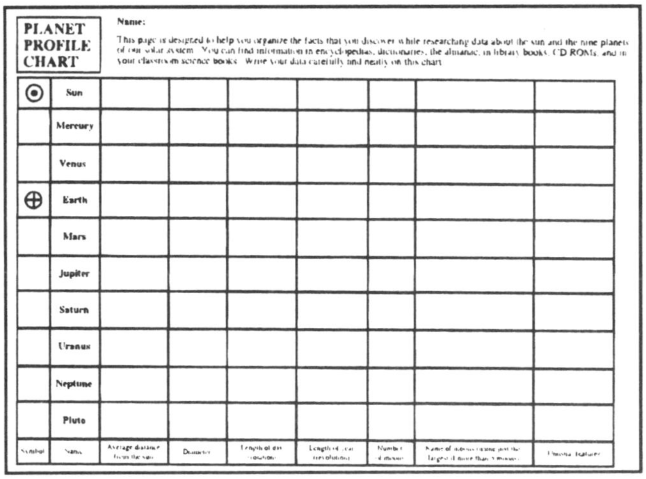

PLANET PROFILE CHART

Name:

This page is designed to help you organize the facts that you discover while researching data about the sun and the nine planets of our solar system. You can find information in encyclopedias, dictionaries, the almanac, in library books, CD ROMs, and in your classroom science books. Write your data carefully and neatly on this chart.

Symbol	Name	Average distance from the sun	Diameter	Length of day (rotation)	Length of year (revolution)	Number of moons	[illegible]	Unusual features
⊙	Sun							
	Mercury							
	Venus							
⊕	Earth							
	Mars							
	Jupiter							
	Saturn							
	Uranus							
	Neptune							
	Pluto							

Extensions

Use the information about the planets to make a series of "Planet Books" that describe the characteristics of each planet. Illustrate the books with drawings, magazine illustrations, or photographs.

Have groups of students use the information on their Planet Profile Chart to create five challenging math problems. Have them trade Planet Profile Charts and problems with other groups and solve them.

PLANET PROFILE CHART

Name: ____________________

This page is designed to help you organize the facts that you discover while researching data about the sun and the nine planets of our solar system. You can find information in encyclopedias, dictionaries, the almanac, in library books, CD ROMs, and in your classroom science books. Write your data carefully and neatly on this chart.

Symbol	Name	Average distance from the sun	Diameter	Length of day (rotation)	Length of year (revolution)	Number of moons	Name of moons (name just the largest if more than 5 moons)	Unusual features
☉	**Sun**							
	Mercury							
	Venus							
⊕	**Earth**							
	Mars							
	Jupiter							
	Saturn							
	Uranus							
	Neptune							
	Pluto							

Note: Reproduce pages 20 and 48 for students doing this activity.

Where is Planet X?

It has been suggested that the unusual motion of the outer planets could be caused by the gravity of a yet undiscovered planet - Planet X - the tenth planet in our solar system. Although this is only speculation, it is possible to use existing information about the planets to predict the likely distance Planet X would be from the sun.

During this activity, students will use information on the Astrofacts page to graph the distance the known planets are away from the sun. They will then extend the graph to predict where a possible tenth planet - Planet X- might be located.

Hints, Tips, and Suggestions

Ask your students to follow the dircctions on the Planet X activity page and plot the location of the planets on the graph. Then ask them to connect the outer planets with a curved line and extend it until the line crosses the Planet X line on the grid. The approximate distance Planet X is from the sun can be found on the vertical axis of the graph.

Extensions

Calculate how long it would take for light from the sun (traveling at 300,000 kilometers per second) to reach Earth. Then calculate how long it would take to reach Planet X.

Although its existence had been mathematically predicted a hundred years before, the planet Pluto wasn't discovered until 1930. Students might want to research how this discovery happened.

Where is Planet X?

Use this grid and information from the Astrofacts page to graph the distance each planet is away from the sun. When you are done, connect the outer planets with a curved line and extend the line until it crosses the line for Planet X. If a tenth planet exists, its approximate distance from the sun can be found on the vertical axis of the graph.

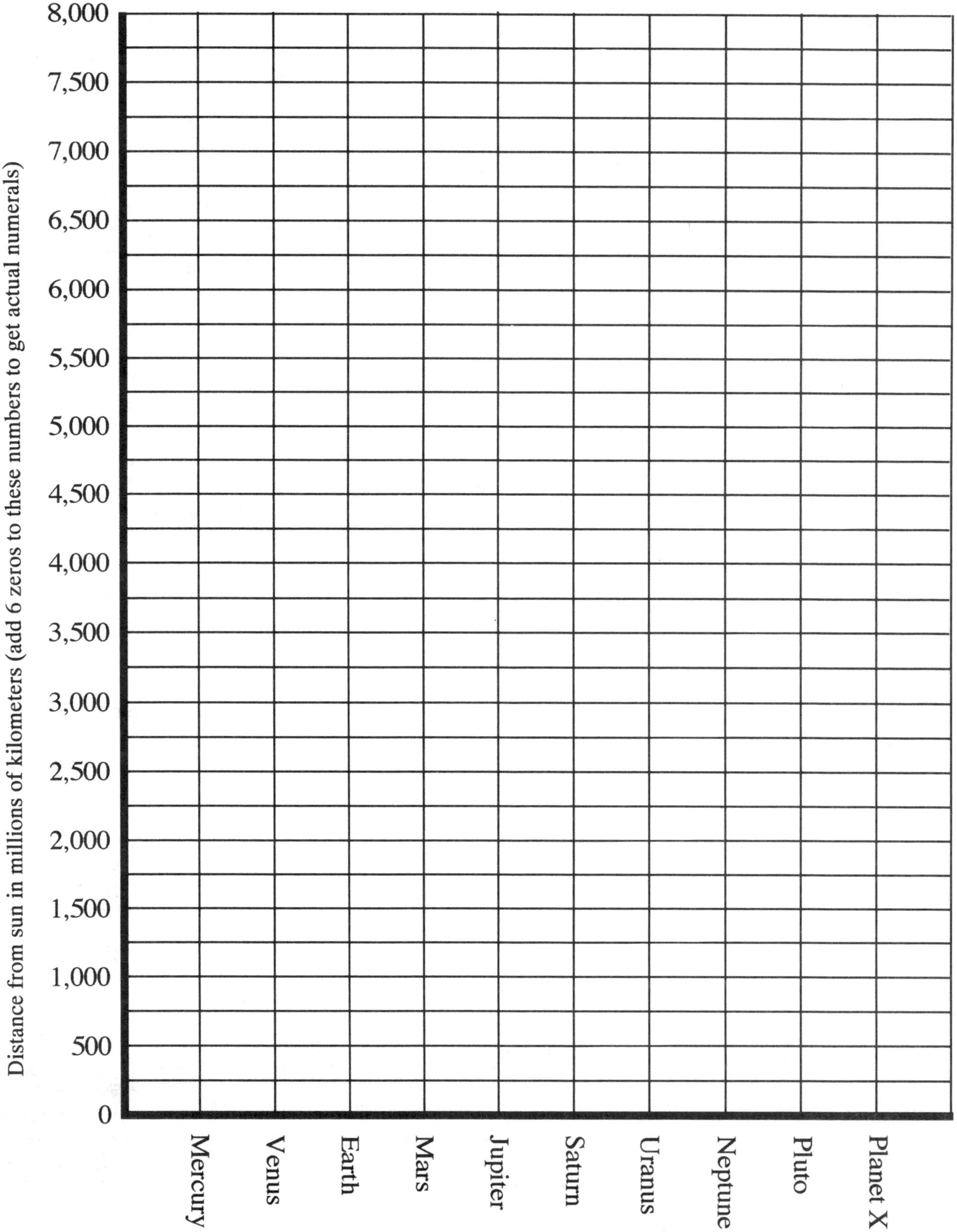

Note: Reproduce pages 22, 23, and 47 for students doing this activity.

Making Planets to Scale

Illustrations of our solar system cannot do justice to the gigantic sizes and enormous distances that are involved. Most drawings depict the planets as being close to the sun and to each other when, in actuality, they are incredible distances apart. Only by making a scale model can students get a feeling for their true relative sizes and distances.

Students will use information from the Astrofacts page (page 48) to calculate the scale size of the sun and the planets as well as their relative distances from each other. They will use their calculations to make scale models of the planets and the sun from clay and a balloon.

Hints and Tips

Many of the numbers the students will be dealing with are too large to fit in a calculator. This activity presents the opportunity to teach your students alternative strategies for dividing and multiplying numbers that contain trailing zeros.

Have your students make the scale models of the planets first, before calculating their scale distances from the sun. Ask a few students to pretend they are the planet Mercury and physically place themselves at a scale distance away from the balloon sun. (Most students will crowd around the balloon because that is the way the orbit of Mercury is depicted in scientific illustrations.) Then have them calculate the actual scale distance (it is about 9 meters!) and compare it to their predictions.

Extensions

Using a metric trundle wheel, or having the students take meter-long steps, place the first four planets at their scale distance away from the sun.

Change the scale to one centimeter = 6,500 kilometers and draw the new and larger planets on cardstock. Staple the cards to sticks and place the cards along a long, straight road at their actual scale distances from the sun. (Note: One mile is equal to about 1.6 kilometers.)

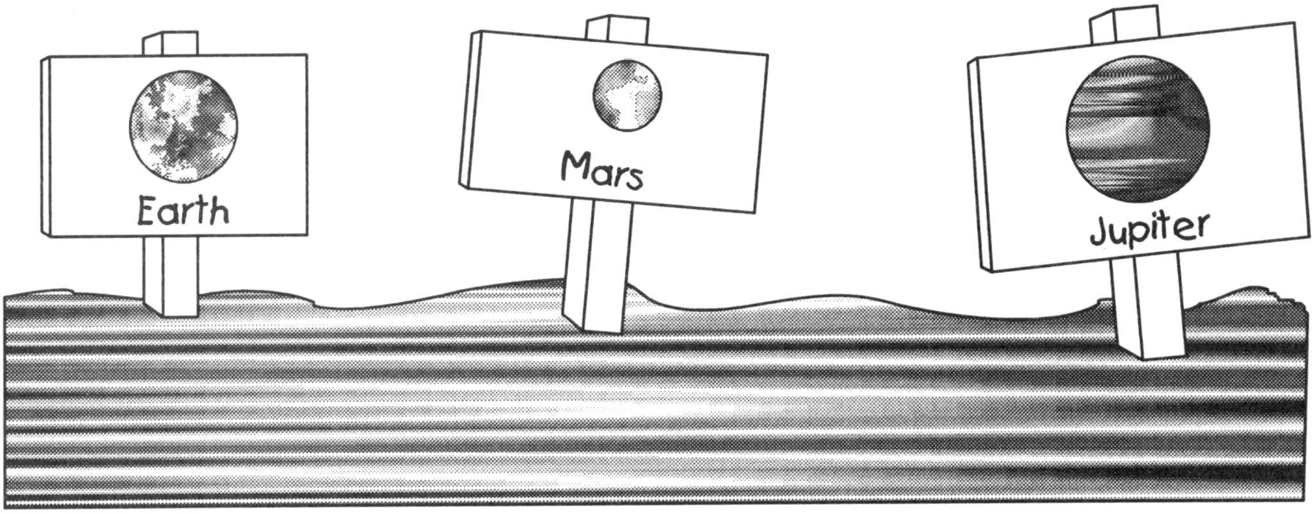

Making Planets to Scale

Student Activity

It is difficult to imagine the actual size of the planets of our solar system and the tremendous distances between them. A good way to visualize these is to construct a scale model.

> Here is the scale you will use: **1 millimeter = 6500 kilometers**
> (That is the same as the thickness of the wire on an ordinary paperclip equaling about 1/5 the circumference of the Earth.)
>
> To make your scale model you will need:
> - modeling clay
> - measuring tools (page 47)
> - Astrofacts Chart (page 48)
> - Solar System Data Chart (page 23)
> - round balloon
> - calculator

First, assemble the measuring tools according to the directions on that page, then complete these two tasks.

1. Calculate the scale size of each of the planets and the sun. Make scale models of them using clay and a balloon.

2. Calculate the scale distance between the planets and the sun.

The Astrofacts page contains all the data you will need to solve your problems. The Solar System Data Chart will help you organize your work. The measuring tools will help you accurately construct scale models of the planets and the sun.

Challenges: Choose one and try to solve it.

1. Place the scale model of Mercury at its scale distance away from the model of the sun.

2. Calculate how long it takes for light from the sun to reach each of the planets.

Solar System Data Chart

Scale: 1 millimeter = 6500 kilometers

object	actual diameter	scale diameter	actual distance from the sun	scale distance from the sun	time for light to travel to the planet
Sun					
Mercury					
Venus					
Earth					
Mars					
Jupiter					
Saturn					
Uranus					
Neptune					
Pluto					

To do:

1. Calculate the scale size of each of these planets and the sun. Make scale models of them using clay and a balloon.
2. Calculate the scale distances between the planets and the sun.
3. Do the challenge of your choice.

Hints:

The answers on your calculator will be in either millimeters (diameter and distance calculations) or seconds (light travel calculations). Remember, there are 10 millimeters in one centimeter, 1000 millimeters in one meter, 60 seconds in a minute, 60 minutes in an hour, and 24 hours in a day.

There will be a lot of zeros in your calculations. Ask someone how to eliminate some of them before entering numbers in the calculator.

Note: Reproduce pages 25 and 48 for students doing this activity.

Birthdays in Space

A year is defined as the time it takes a planet to travel once around the sun. A year on Mercury is quite short compared to an Earth year, while a year on Pluto is the equivalent of several lifetimes. This means that given the same span of time, a student living on Mercury would technically be about four times older than a student on Earth, and a student living on Pluto would still be an infant compared to the other two.

During this activity, students will use information from the Astrofacts page to calculate what their age would be if they lived on different planets.

Hints and Tips

In order to do the activity, students will have to convert the revolution period of planets into days. In doing so, have them all use the same constant - 365.25 days = one Earth year - in their calculations.

Although the calculations in this activity are fairly easy, the use of a calculator will speed up the activity. Also, some students may need a calendar in order to solve the challenge on this activity page.

Extensions

What would life be like if everything done on Earth was done proportionally according to the length of the year on another planet?
For example:

- How long would the school year be?
- How long would summer last?
- How many days would be in a month (assuming 12 months in a year)?

Birthdays in Space

Student Activity

A year is the amount of time it takes for a planet to circle the sun once. Every time you celebrate a birthday, you've ridden the Earth once around the sun.

A year on Earth is 365.25 days long, but the length of a year on other planets changes with the distance the planet is away from the sun. For example, Mercury zips around the sun once every 88 days while Pluto makes the same trip in a little less than 250 Earth years!

So, how old would you be if you lived on another planet? You can calculate how many years old you would be on any other planet. Just follow the directions and fill in this chart with your answers.

Planet	Birthday Calculations	Age on this Planet
Mercury	$\frac{\text{Your Earth age}}{\text{Length of planet's year in days}} \times 365$	years
Venus	$\frac{\text{Your Earth age}}{\text{Length of planet's year in days}} \times 365$	years
Earth	Your Earth age X 1	years
Mars	$\frac{\text{Your Earth age}}{\text{Length of planet's year in days}} \times 365$	years
Jupiter	$\left(\frac{\text{Your Earth age}}{\text{Length of planet's year in days}} \times 365\right) \times 12$	months
Saturn	$\left(\frac{\text{Your Earth age}}{\text{Length of planet's year in days}} \times 365\right) \times 12$	months
Uranus	$\left(\frac{\text{Your Earth age}}{\text{Length of planet's year in days}} \times 365\right) \times 52$	months
Neptune	$\left(\frac{\text{Your Earth age}}{\text{Length of planet's year in days}} \times 365\right) \times 52$	weeks
Pluto	$\left(\frac{\text{Your Earth age}}{\text{Length of planet's year in days}} \times 365\right) \times 52$	weeks

Challenge:

Choose one planet besides Earth and calculate your exact age by changing the decimal part of a year to months, weeks, and days.

Note: Reproduce page 27 for students doing this activity.

Heavier or Lighter?

When dealing with matter, there is a distinct difference between mass and weight. The mass of an object has to do with the quantity of matter of which it is composed. An object's weight, however, varies with the force of gravity. For example, although the mass of a space traveler visiting the planets of the solar system would not change much during the trip, the traveler's weight would fluctuate according to the force of gravity on a particular planet.

During this activity, students will use information on the student activity page to calculate their weight on different planets.

Hints, Tips, and Suggestions

Some students may have difficulty translating decimals written as words into decimals writen as numerals.

When astronauts from the U.S.A. walked on the moon in the 1960's and 70's, they experienced about 1/6 the gravity of Earth. This meant that their spacesuits and life support equipment weighed far less on the moon than on Earth and the astronauts could jump higher and hop farther using their “Earth muscles.” This difference in gravity had to be taken into consideration in the design of lunar landing craft and during the training of the astronauts.

Extensions

The force of Earth's gravity varies with the amount of matter beneath the observer. There are places on Earth where gravity is stronger or weaker than normal. These locations affect the orbit of artificial satellites. Some of your students might want to research to find out the location of a few of those places.

Earth's tides are controlled by the combined gravitational forces of the sun and the moon. Have your students research to find out what causes the tides and what effect tidal forces have on the Earth (they are gradually slowing down Earth's rotation period).

Research to find out what special astronaut training was devised to give Apollo astronauts an idea of what the moon's gravity would be like. Also find out about NASA's efforts to establish a permanent scientific base on the moon.

Heavier or Lighter?

Student Activity

Have you ever wondered how much you would weigh if you lived on a different planet? Would you weigh more than you do now if you lived on Mars rather than Earth? Well, you can use multiplication and decimals to find out.

Although your mass - the stuff that your body is made up of would be the same on all the planets, your weight would be heavier or lighter depending on the planet's force of gravity.

For example, a person who weighs 45 kg (about 100 pounds) on Earth would weigh about 1260 kg (2800 pounds) if they could somehow stand on the surface of the sun ("Ooh, ouch!").

To find out how much you would weigh on each of the planets of the solar system, perform these calculations.

Your weight on:

Mercury = Earth weight X thirty-eight hundredths	
Venus = Earth weight X ninety-one hundredths	
Earth = Earth weight X one	
Mars = Earth weight X thirty-eight hundredths	
Jupiter = Earth weight X two and six tenths	
Saturn = Earth weight X one and one tenth	
Uranus = Earth weight X nine tenths	
Neptune = Earth weight X one and two tenths	
Pluto = Earth weight X eight-hundredths	

Challenges:

- On which planet would you probably be a champion high jumper? ______________
- On which planet would you find it difficult to stand up and move around? ______________
- Gravity on the moon is about 1/6 as strong as Earth's. How much would you weigh on the moon? ______________________________

Part 3

Stars and Space

Background

Although the stars appear fixed in the heavens, we know that is not the case. The universe is in constant motion and stars are moving away from each other at tremendous speeds. If you could visit Earth a million years from now you would undoubtedly see a completely different arrangement of stars than you are used to.

Stars are rated on a magnitude scale according to the intensity of their light. The original scale was created in 250 B.C. by Hipparchus, a Greek astronomer. He rated the brightest stars as 1 (first magnitude) and the dimmest stars as 6 (sixth magnitude). With the invention of the telescope, scientists were forced to change the scale, adding more magnitudes in each direction, and even creating negative magnitudes for the very brightest objects.

The star Sirius, located in the constellation Canis Major, is the brightest of all the stars seen from Earth. It is rated on the Hipparchus scale as magnitude -1.5 and is 8.7 light years (87 trillion km) away. Seven of the brightest stars in the northern hemisphere are located near Sirius. The Constellation and Star Finder in this section will help your students locate them as well as seven other first magnitude stars that are visible in the northern hemisphere.

Lastly, consider these facts about distances in space: If our sun was the size of an apple, Earth would be a grain of salt nearly 9 meters away. To reach Alpha Centauri, the next closest star besides our sun, you would have to travel another 2400 km from your "apple" sun. And to reach Sirius, you would have to add another 3000 km to the trip. Perhaps that is why space is called space...and not stuff!

Note: Reproduce page 30 for students doing this activity.

String - Art Comet

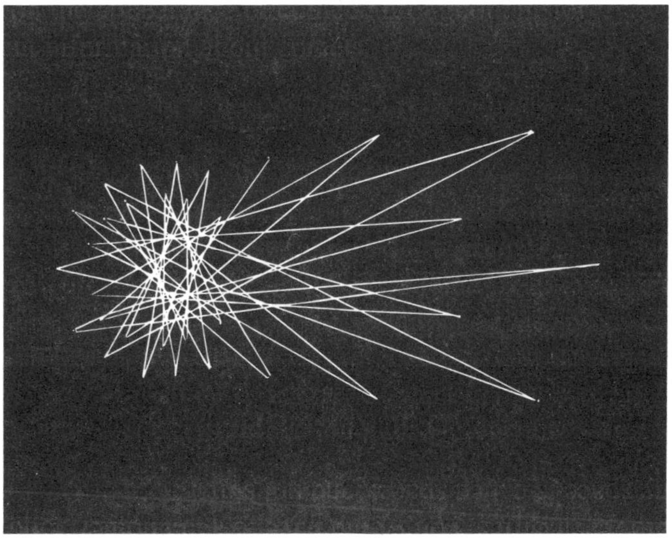

Background

Most comets originate in a huge cloud of dust and ice that surround our solar system at a distance of several thousand times its radius. They are thought to be the most ancient objects in the solar system, changing little since they first formed over 4 billion years ago.

Although both comets and planets orbit the sun, they differ from each other in a number of ways. Most planets orbit in a single plane, like pepperoni on a pizza while comets orbit in both directions and in many different planes. Both planets and comets shine by reflecting sunlight, but when comets are close to the sun, their gases are excited by ultraviolet radiation and give off light just like a fluorescent light.

Comets travel at various speeds - going faster as they near the sun and slowing down as they travel away from it. Despite the myths associated with them, comets do not streak across the sky like meteorites. Weeks and months may pass before a comet completes its swing around the sun.

Some comets are frequent visitors to the solar system while others are once-in-a-lifetime events. Encke's comet revolves in a circular orbit around the sun and appears every 3.5 years. Tuttle's comet visits the sun every 14 years, and Halley's comet, perhaps the most famous of them all, reappears once every 76 years.

Making a String Comet

Your students will be using needles and thread to make their comets. In order to understand the problems your students may encounter, make your own string-art comet before assigning the activity to your students. Go over the directions on page 30 carefully with your students before they begin. You may want to have them review counting by odd and even numbers before you begin. Provide needle threaders for children having difficulty threading a needle.

Extensions

- Create patterns for string-art stars.
- Research and report on the appearance of comets throughout history.
- Report the most recent information about comets.

String - Art Comet

1. Glue this page to half of a file folder and glue black construction paper to the other side of the file folder. With the printed side up, poke holes with a push pin wherever there is a dot or a circle. Thread a needle with white thread and push it down through hole #1. Pull the thread all the way through and tape the free end onto this side of the pattern. Push the needle up through hole #3, down through hole #5, following the odd numbers until you get to the end. Rethread the needle as needed, taping the free end of the thread to this side of the pattern.

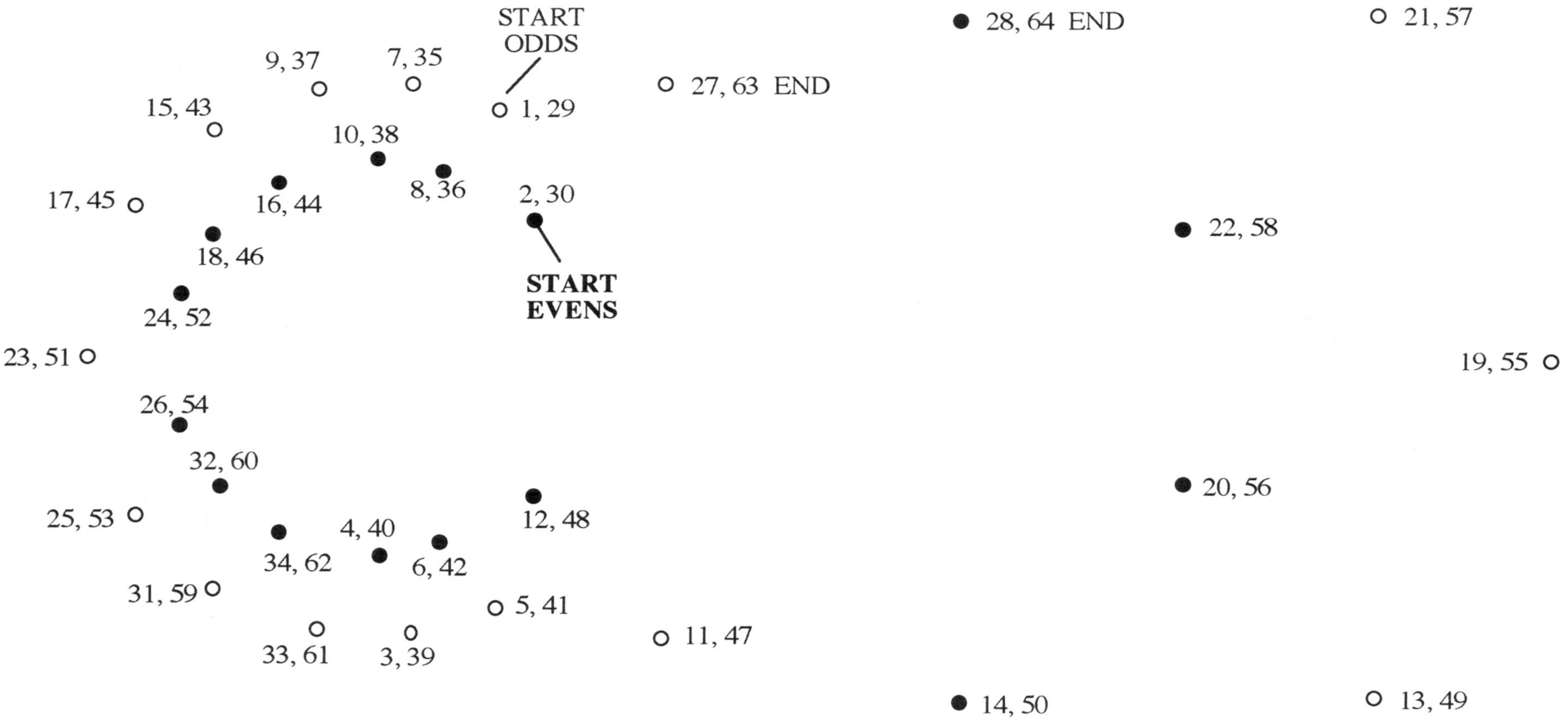

2. Thread a needle with a different color thread and push it down through hole #2. Pull the thread all the way through and tape the free end onto this side of the pattern. Push the needle up through hole #4, down through hole #6, following the even numbers until you get to the end. Rethread the needle as needed, taping the free end of the thread to this side of the pattern.

Note: Reproduce page 33 for students doing this activity.

Celestial Timepiece

The constellations that surround Polaris, the north star, are the only ones visible in the northern hemisphere every night of the year. Three of them - Cassiopeia, Ursa Major, and Ursa Minor - are especially easy to recognize. Ursa Major, the Big Dipper, is probably the easiest of the three to locate.

The Big Dipper appears to revolve around the North Star once each day. Of course, the constellations aren't actually moving, rather it is Earth's rotation that makes them appear to move. However, this apparent motion is so predictable that if you know the month of the year, the position of the Big Dipper can tell you the time.

Provide practice using the timepiece by making a large drawing of the Big Dipper and positioning it in the front of the room. Rotate the drawing in positions similar to those shown on the timepiece. For each position, tell the students the month and have them use their celestial timepieces to tell you what time it should be. Occasionally provide the students with the time and have them tell you the month. (This can be done by placing the time in the notch and turning the entire celestial timepiece until the position of the Big Dipper matches the one on the board.)

Hints, Tips, and Suggestions

Conserve file folders by having the students rough cut the two parts of the Celestial Timepiece before gluing them down.

The Big Dipper can be used to point out the location of several first magnitude stars. If you follow the arc of the handle away from the Big Dipper, it points to the first magnitude star.

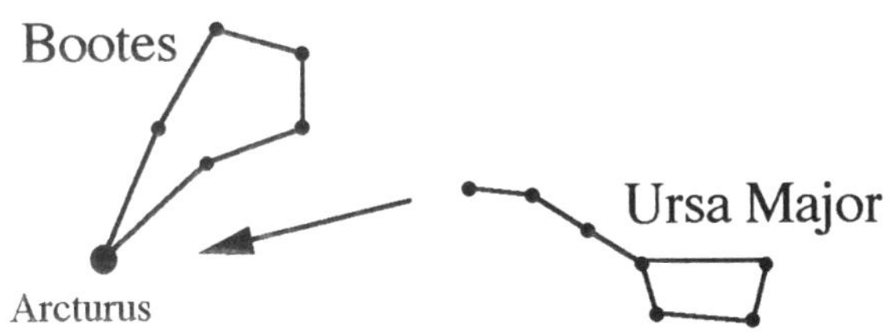

Follow the arc of the handle away from Ursa Major to find the first magnitude star Arcturus in the constellation Bootes.

Figure 1

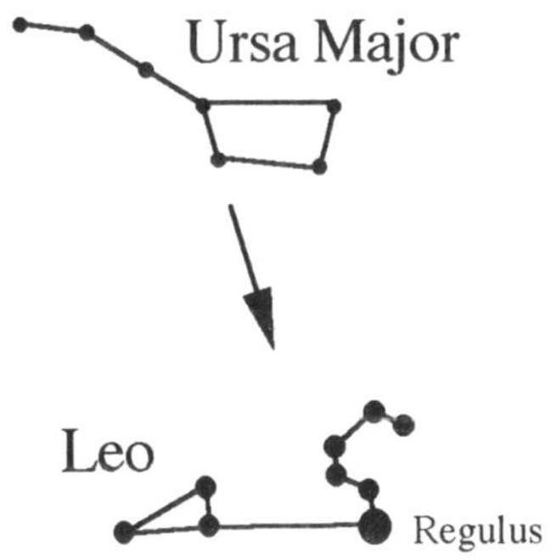

Follow the arc of the handle towards Ursa Major to find the first magnitude star Regulus in the constellation Leo.

Figure 2

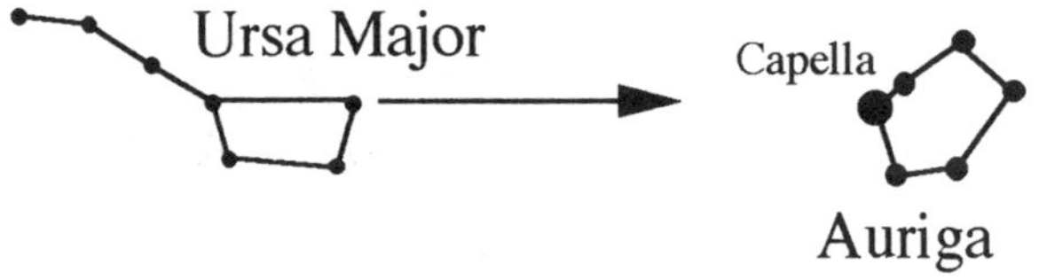

An imaginary line drawn across the top of the pan of the Big Dipper points to the first magnitude star Capella in the constellation Auriga.

Figure 3

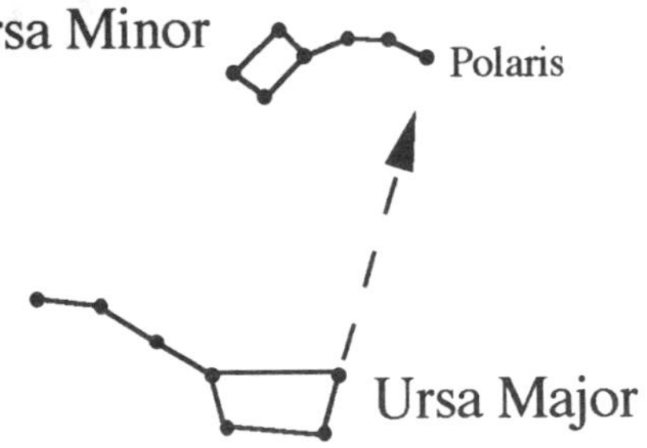

A line drawn through the end stars in Ursa Major points Polaris, the North Star.

Figure 4

Extensions

Have students research the Greek and Roman myths surrounding the polar constellations - Cassiopeia, Ursa Major, Ursa Minor, Cepheus, and Perseus.

Ask your students to surmise how ancient people could tell the seasons of the year from the position of the Big Dipper. (The position of the handle tells the seasons. The handle points upwards in Summer, to the left in Spring, downwards in Winter, and to the right in Autumn.)

Have students read ***Follow the Drinking Gourd*** by Jeanette Winter or ***Her Seven Brothers*** by Paul Goble and report on the role the Big Dipper plays in these stories.

Celestial Timepiece

All night long the Big Dipper appears to revolve around the North Star. Its motion is so predictable that if you know the month of the year, the position of the Big Dipper can tell you the correct time.

To make a Celestial Timepiece that you can use to tell the time, you will need the following materials:

- the patterns on this page
- half of a file folder
- scissors and a push pin
- paper fastener
- glue stik

1. Glue both parts of the timepiece to half of a file folder. Carefully cut them out on the outside lines.

2. With the push pin, poke a hole in the center of each part. Place the smaller part on top of the larger part and connect them with a paper fastener.

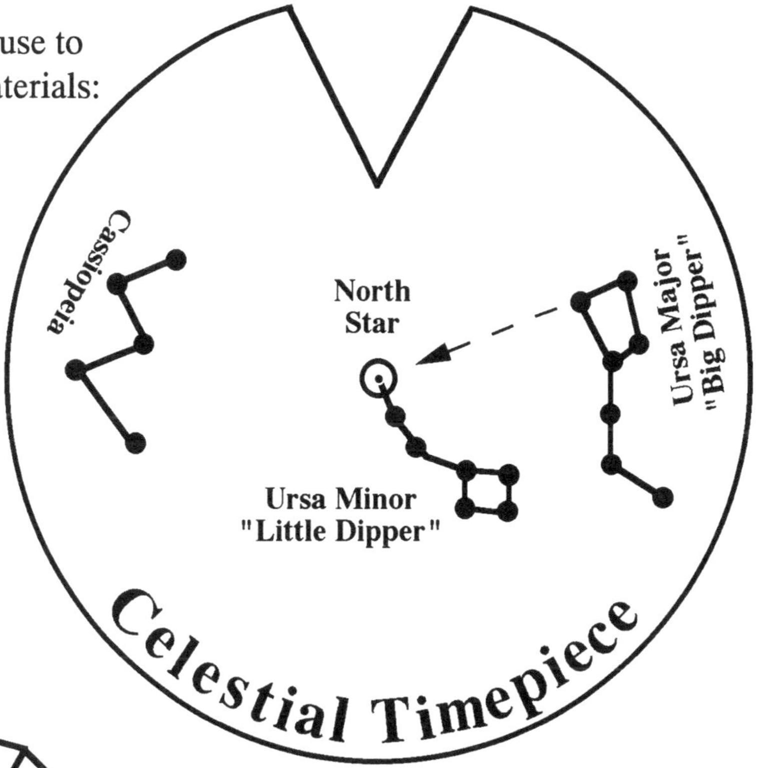

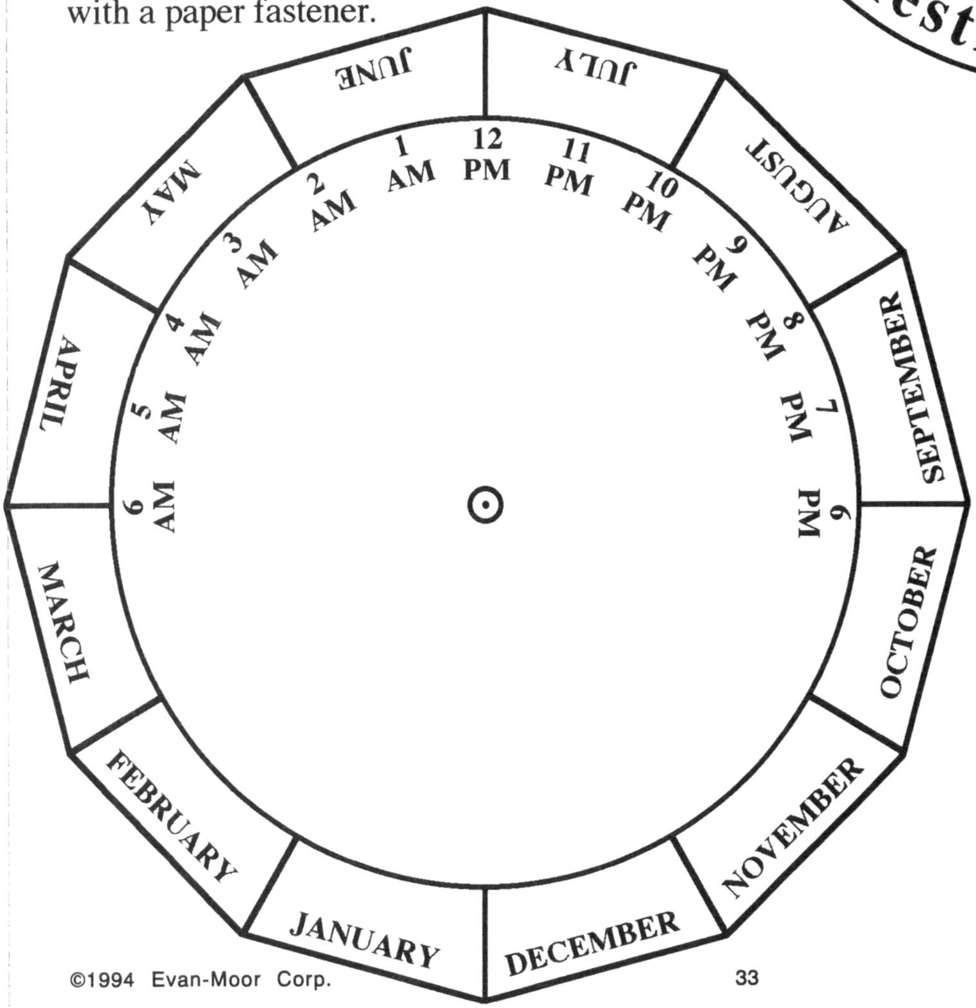

Using the Celestial Timepiece
(Cut this out and glue it to the back of your Celestial Timepiece.)

Outside at night, face the North Star and locate the Big Dipper.

Find the current month on the outside ring of the Celestial Timepiece. Turn the entire clock so that the current month is at the bottom. Hold that month between your thumb and first finger.

Rotate the inner wheel until the drawings of the Big Dipper and the North Star line up with the current position of the actual stars.

The approximate time is shown in the notch. (If it is summer and you are on Daylight Savings Time, add one hour to the time shown.)

Note: Reproduce pages 35 and 36 for students doing this activity.

No Beginning and No End

There are many things in the universe that the human mind has a problem understanding. For example, some astronomers theorize that the universe has no beginning and no end, but instead stretches on forever in all directions. It is impossible for the mind to conceive of such a thing, but it may be true just the same.

Your students can construct something that the mind cannot conceive of. It technically has no beginning and no end and contains only one continuous surface and one continuous edge. It is called a Mobius loop and the directions for making it and four experiments your students can do with it are on pages 35 and 36.

Hints, Tips, and Suggestions

Larger loops can be made from sheets of newspaper.

Extensions

- Research to find out how the Mobius loop got its name.
- Find out what happens if you twist the loop more than once.
- Research the life of Dutch artist M. C. Escher to find out how he used Mobius loops in his mathematical art.
- Find out if there are any commercial applications for the Mobius loop (conveyor belts and drive belts shaped into Mobius loops will last twice as long).

No Beginning and No End
Student Activity

There are many things in the universe that the human mind has a problem understanding. Here is a chance to make something the mind cannot imagine - an object with only one side.

Materials:
- several 5 cm by 61 cm strips of construction paper
- ruler
- pencil
- scissors
- tape or glue

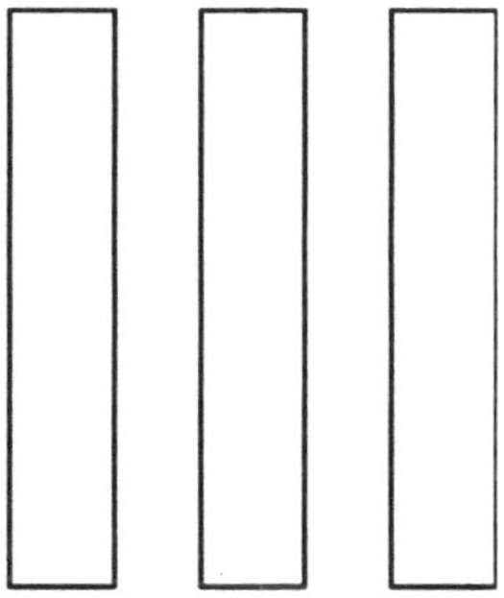

Directions:

1. Take a strip of construction paper and mark an X on each end.

   Roll the strip into a ring and glue the two ends together. Do the same thing with two more strips.

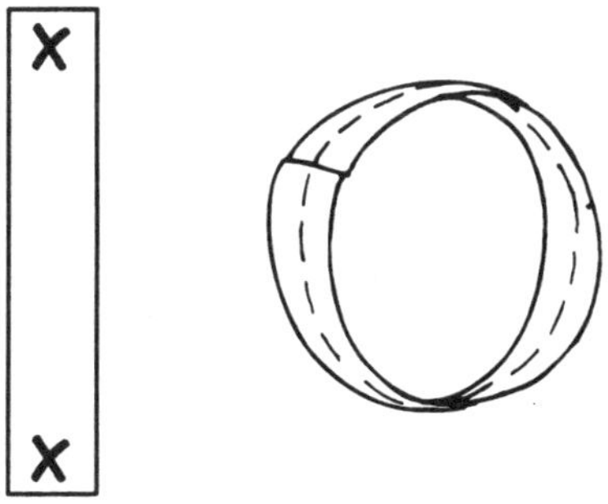

Make 3.

2. Take another strip of construction paper and mark an X on each end. Twist one end of the strip over so that the X on that end will be facing the opposite direction of the X on the other end.

   Bring the two ends of the twisted strip together so the X's touch each other. Glue the overlapping ends of the strip together. Do the same thing with two more strips.

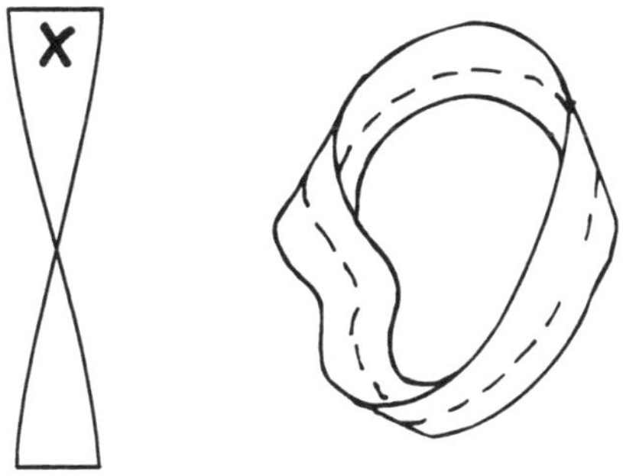

Make 3.

Experiment #1

How many surfaces do the loops have?

With a pencil, put an X somewhere on the outside of a "regular" loop. Starting at that mark, draw a continuous line around the loop until you get back to the X. How many surfaces does the regular loop have? Is only one side of the loop marked?

Now, do the same thing with one of the "twisted" loops. Start at the X and draw around the loop until you return to the X. Surprise! This line is twice as long as the line on the regular loop. If you look carefully, you will see that it is drawn on all sides of the paper.

The twisted loop is called a Mobius loop. If you trace it with your finger, you will find it has only one continuous surface and one continuous edge. In fact, it is the only thing on Earth that has only one side and one edge.

Experiment #2

What will happen if you cut the loops?

Poke a point of your scissors into the center of the side of a regular loop and cut all the way around down the center line. Do the same kind of "down the center" cut with a Mobius loop. How are the new loops alike and different? Draw a line around these loops as you did before.

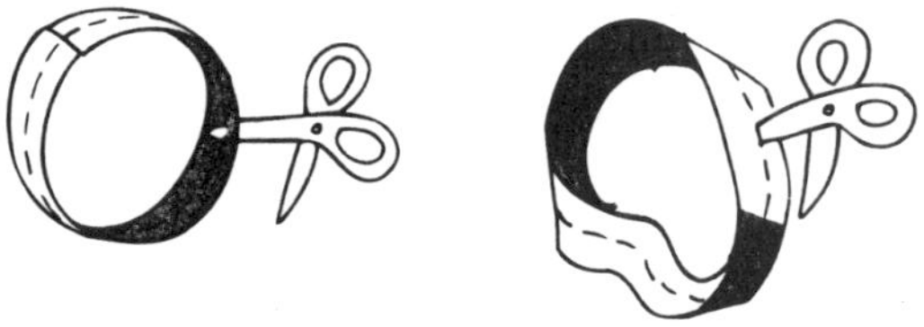

Experiment #3

What will happen if you cut near the edge?

Poke the point of your scissors into a regular loop closer to one edge than the other. Cut the loop all the way around until you get back to the beginning, but try to stay the same distance from the edge the entire time. Do the same thing with a Mobius loop, but before completing this cut, predict what the result will be. How are the two loops alike and different?

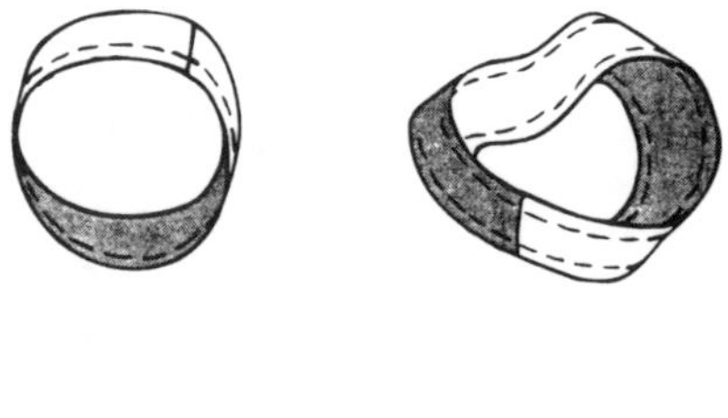

Experiment #4

Put two loops together.

This activity has a surprising result. Glue a regular loop and a Mobius loop together so they cross each other at right angles - like a street intersection. Draw a center line around both loops and cut the loops down their center lines. Unfold the resulting loop.

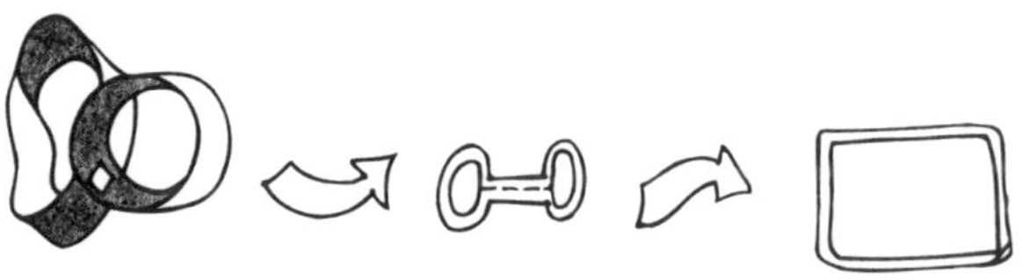

Does the same thing happen when two regular loops or Mobius loops are glued together and cut the same way?

Note: Reproduce pages 38 through 41 to use with this activity.

What's Special About Sirius?

Background

The star Sirius is part of the constellation Canis Major (which means the big dog). It is the brightest object in the nighttime sky. It first appears in mid-November and retires behind the glare of the morning sun in mid-April. At 8.7 light years away, Sirius is the third closest star to Earth (the closest is our sun followed by Alpha Centauri), and the closest in the Northern Hemisphere.

Sirius is actually a double star. Its counterpart, a white dwarf star hidden by the glare of Sirius, has a diameter slightly larger than three times that of Earth and is nearly as massive as our sun. The gaseous matter of this tiny star is so dense that 15 milliliters of it would weigh as much as an automobile!

About the Activities

There are three activities in this section which are associated with Sirius and the Orion Constellation. Your students can make a device which will help you locate Sirius if you know the date and the time (page 38). They can attach to it a map of the first magnitude stars that surround Orion (page 39). They can also make a three-dimensional model of the Orion constellation and the star Sirius (pages 40 and 41).

Hints, Tips, and Suggestions

Have your students construct the Sirius Star Finder according to the directions on the page. The star chart printed on "The Best and the Brightest," page 39, may be glued to the back of the Star Finder. It shows the location of eight first magnitude stars that surround Orion.

To use the Star Finder, place the time of your observation opposite the date. Face south and hold the Star Finder upright. The arrow on the Star Finder will point in the general direction of Sirius and the constellation Canis Major. To use the finder as a clock, rotate the dial until the arrow points towards Sirius. The approximate time can be found next to the date of the observation.

Extensions

- Find out how the star Sirius got its nickname as "the dog star."
- Research and report on the legends associated with Orion and the constellations that surround it.

Sirius Star Finder

and Orion Constellation Locator

• Glue this page to thin cardstock or half of a file folder. Cut the parts out on the solid outside lines.

• Punch the center holes on both parts of the star finder with a push pin. Widen the holes with a sharp pencil point.

• Place the circular part on top of the paddle-shaped base as shown in this drawing. Connect the two parts together with a paper fastener.

Be sure the circular piece is free to rotate.

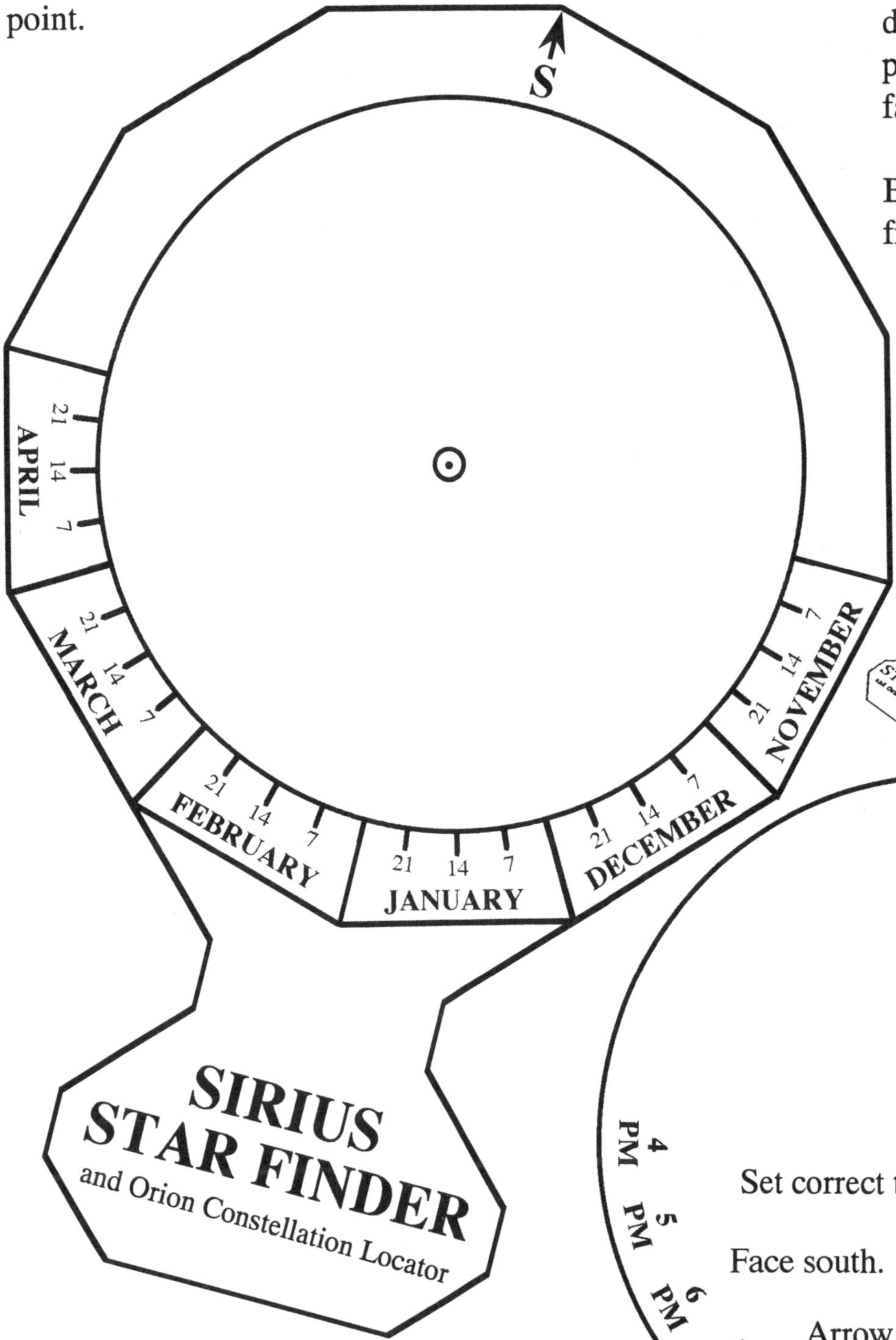

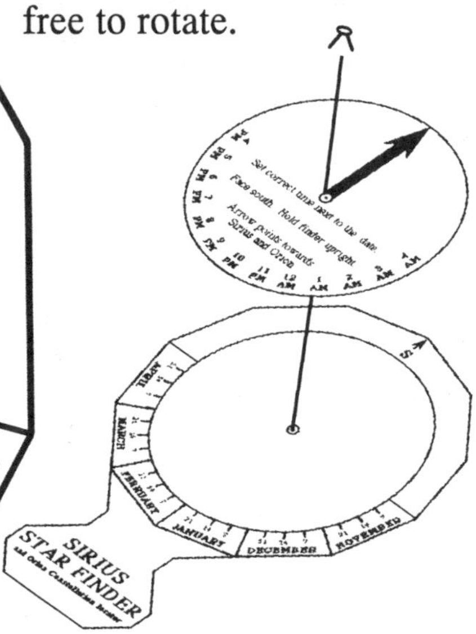

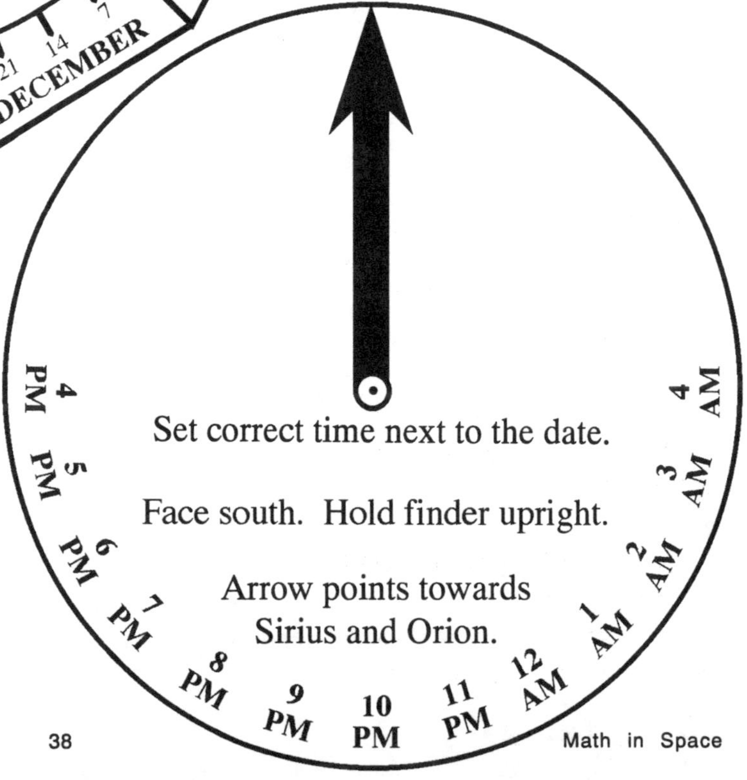

The Best and the Brightest

Astronomers classify stars according to their brilliance. The most brilliant stars in the night sky are called first magnitude stars. Sirius is a first magnitude star. In fact, Sirius is the brightest of all the stars visible from Earth.

These are the 10 brightest stars in the order of their brilliance:

1. Sirius
2. Vega
3. Capella
4. Arcturus
5. Rigel
6. Procyon
7. Altair
8. Betelgeuse
9. Aldebaran
10. Pollux

Out of the ten brightest stars, seven of them are found in and around the Orion constellation.

They are easy to locate. Find all of the first magnitude stars in this drawing. Notice that they sort of form a circle with Betelgeuse at the center.

On a winter night, look for Orion. It is easy to spot because it is the only constellation with three stars in a straight line.

Poke an imaginary compass into Betelgeuse and open it up as far as Sirius. Draw an imaginary circle in the sky with your compass and look for the brightest stars on the circumference of your circle. They are the first magnitude stars shown on this star map.

To get to know these stars and constellations, cut this star map out and glue it to the back of your Sirius star finder. Refer to it when you are out looking for Sirius.

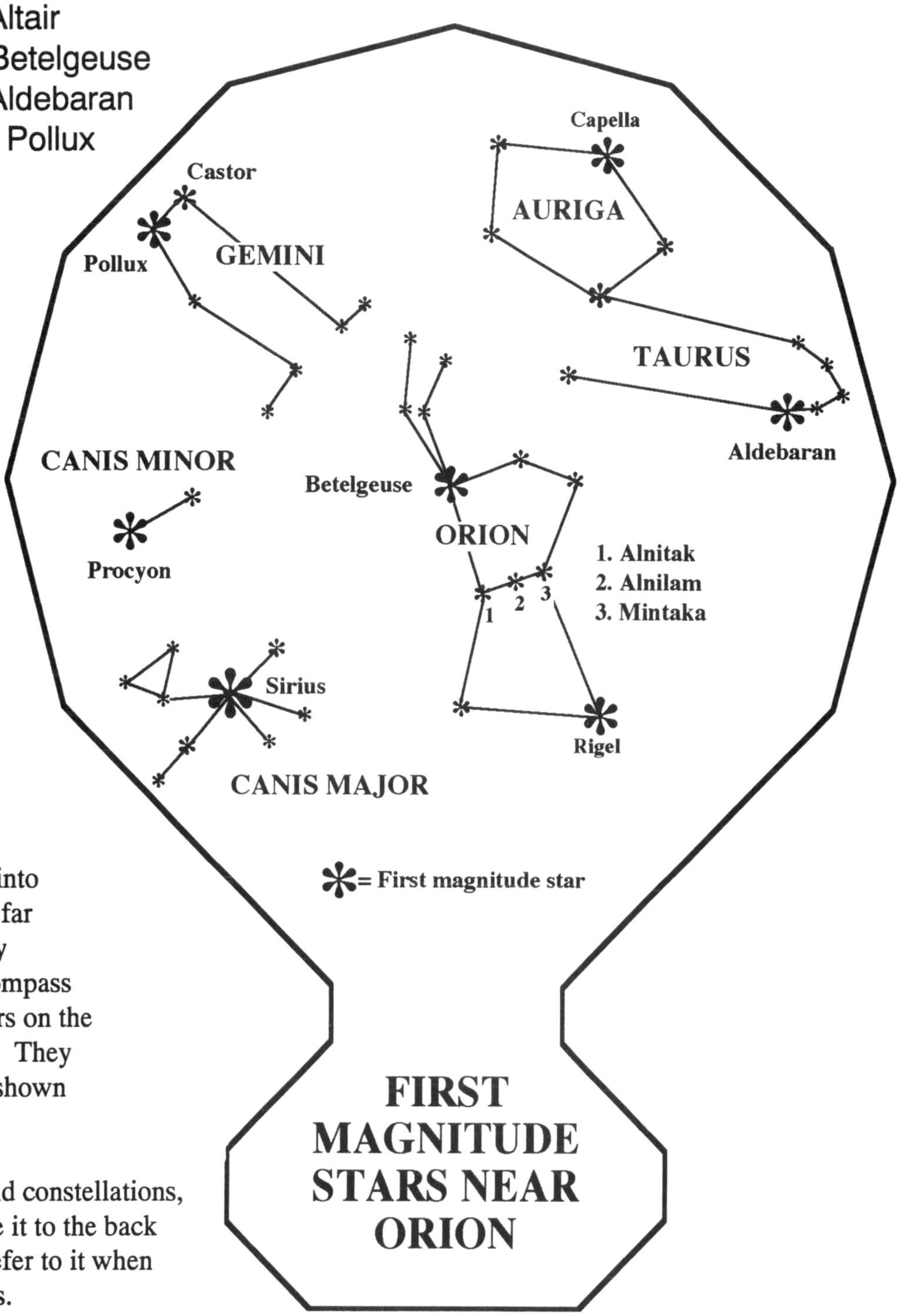

Sirius and the Orion Constellation Star Field

When you look at a constellation in the night sky, the stars appear to be flat against the darkness. But that is not the case. The stars you see are actually great distances apart from each other. You can see this better if you make a 3-D model of a constellation.

You will need:

- scissors
- uncooked spaghetti
- white, red, and blue clay or mini marshmallows
- white glue
- glue stick
- push pin
- black marking pen
- cardboard
- Sirius and the Orion Constellation Star Field

1. Use the glue stick to glue the Sirius and the Orion Constellation Star Field page to a piece of thick cardboard.
2. Use a push pin to poke a hole in the center of each circle that marks the location of a star on the star field.
3. Roll small balls of clay or use small marshmallows to represent the stars. Roll 3 large balls and 5 small balls to the sizes shown at the bottom of this page.
4. Use pieces of spaghetti to support the clay stars. Measure and break the spaghetti pieces to the exact lengths of each support stick as shown on the bottom of this page. Use the black marking pen to color each spaghetti piece black.
5. Put the correct clay star on one end of each piece of spaghetti, as shown below.
6. Put a little white glue into each pin hole. Take the spaghetti sticks one at a time and carefully push the free end into the correct hole on the star field. Try to make each support stick stand up straight. (You may need to hold the support for a short time until the glue begins to set up.) Set the star field aside until the glue dries.

Cut support sticks to this length.

Cut support sticks to this length.	Star Name
12.5 cm	Betelgeuse
11.4 cm	Bellatrix
7 cm	Mintake
6.5 cm	Alnilam
6 cm	Alnitak
2.6 cm	Rigel
2 cm	Saiph
1 cm	Sirius

Star Size

1 cm
Make 3.

.5 cm
Make 5.

Roll clay or mini-marshmallow spheres to these sizes to represent stars in the Orion Constellation. Make all of the stars white except for Betelgeuse (red) and Rigel (blue).

Sirius and the Orion Constellation Star Field

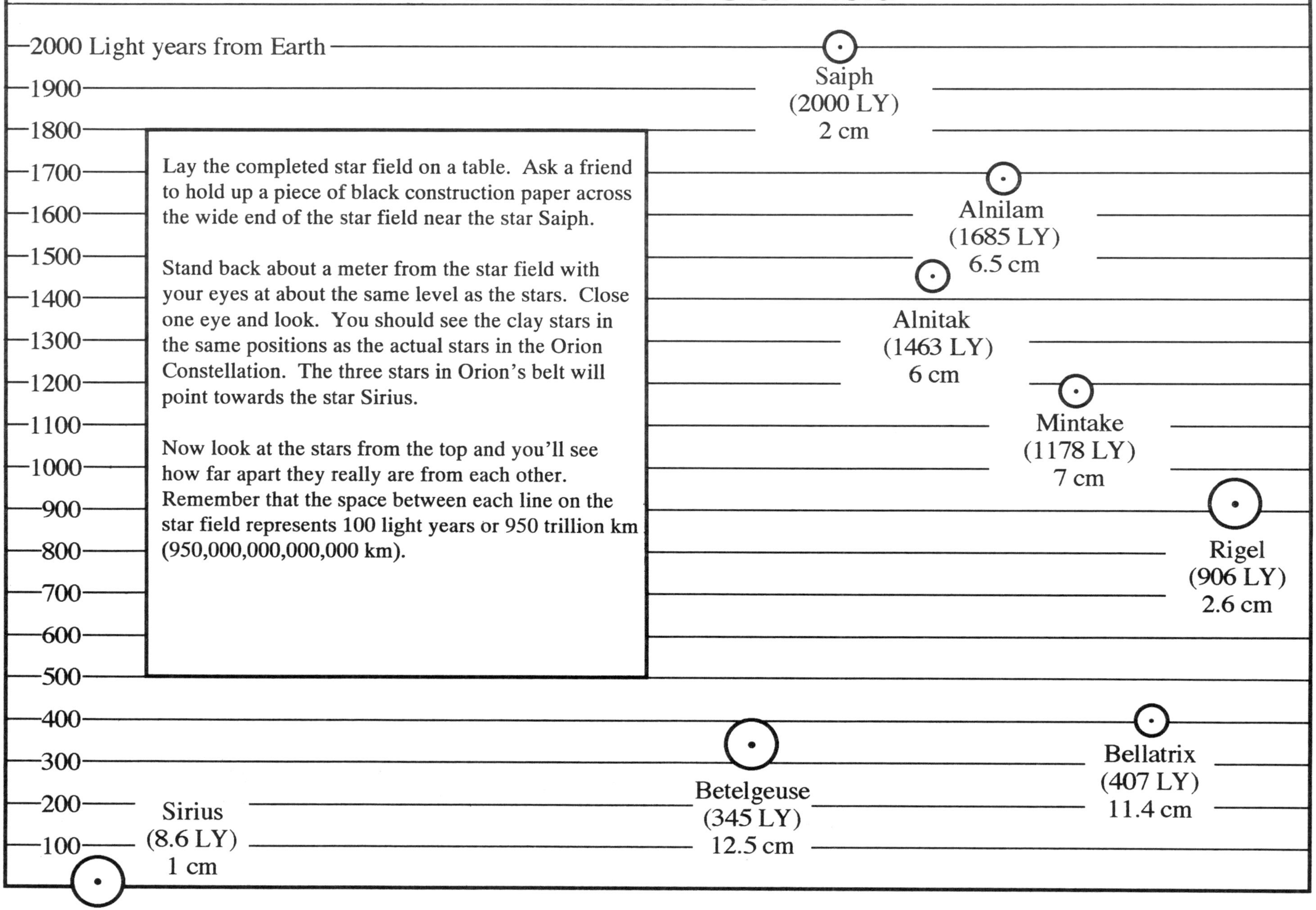

Lay the completed star field on a table. Ask a friend to hold up a piece of black construction paper across the wide end of the star field near the star Saiph.

Stand back about a meter from the star field with your eyes at about the same level as the stars. Close one eye and look. You should see the clay stars in the same positions as the actual stars in the Orion Constellation. The three stars in Orion's belt will point towards the star Sirius.

Now look at the stars from the top and you'll see how far apart they really are from each other. Remember that the space between each line on the star field represents 100 light years or 950 trillion km (950,000,000,000,000 km).

Note: Reproduce pages 43 and 44 for students doing this activity.

Constellation and Star Finder

This device is designed to show the stars as they would appear to an observer at 35 degrees north latitude. Only the brightest stars are shown on part two of the Constellation and Star Finder. These are the stars that are usually visible in light-filled metropolitan areas. The names of the constellations are in bold type while the names of first magnitude stars in those constellations are printed in smaller and lighter type.

Hints, Tips, and Suggestions

The tongue that dips down into the window of the star finder is its most fragile part. Consider reinforcing the hole for the paper fastener with tape or a gummed reinforcer. Stars and constellations hidden beneath the tongue will also be visible in the night sky.

Extensions

- Ask students to use a star map and sketch in some of the missing constellations on their star finder.
- Research the myths and legends that surround various constellations.
- Figure out how to adjust the star finder for someone living in Hawaii or Alaska.

Constellation and Star Finder

Part One

• Glue this page to thin cardstock or half of a file folder. Cut this part of the constellation and star finder out on the solid outside line.

• Punch the center hole with a push pin. Widen the hole with the point of a sharp pencil.

• Assemble the two parts with a paper fastener as shown in the drawing.

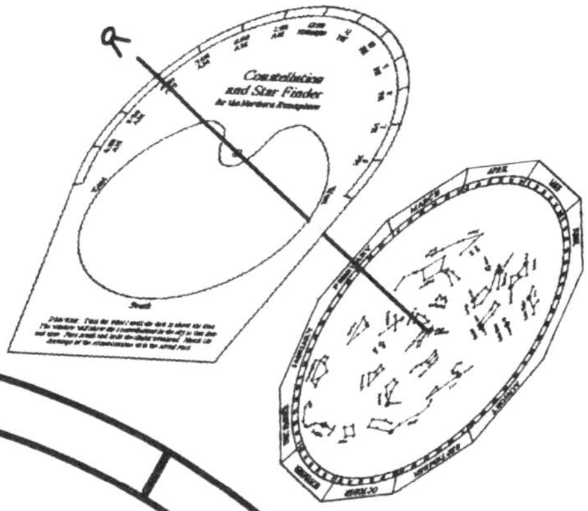

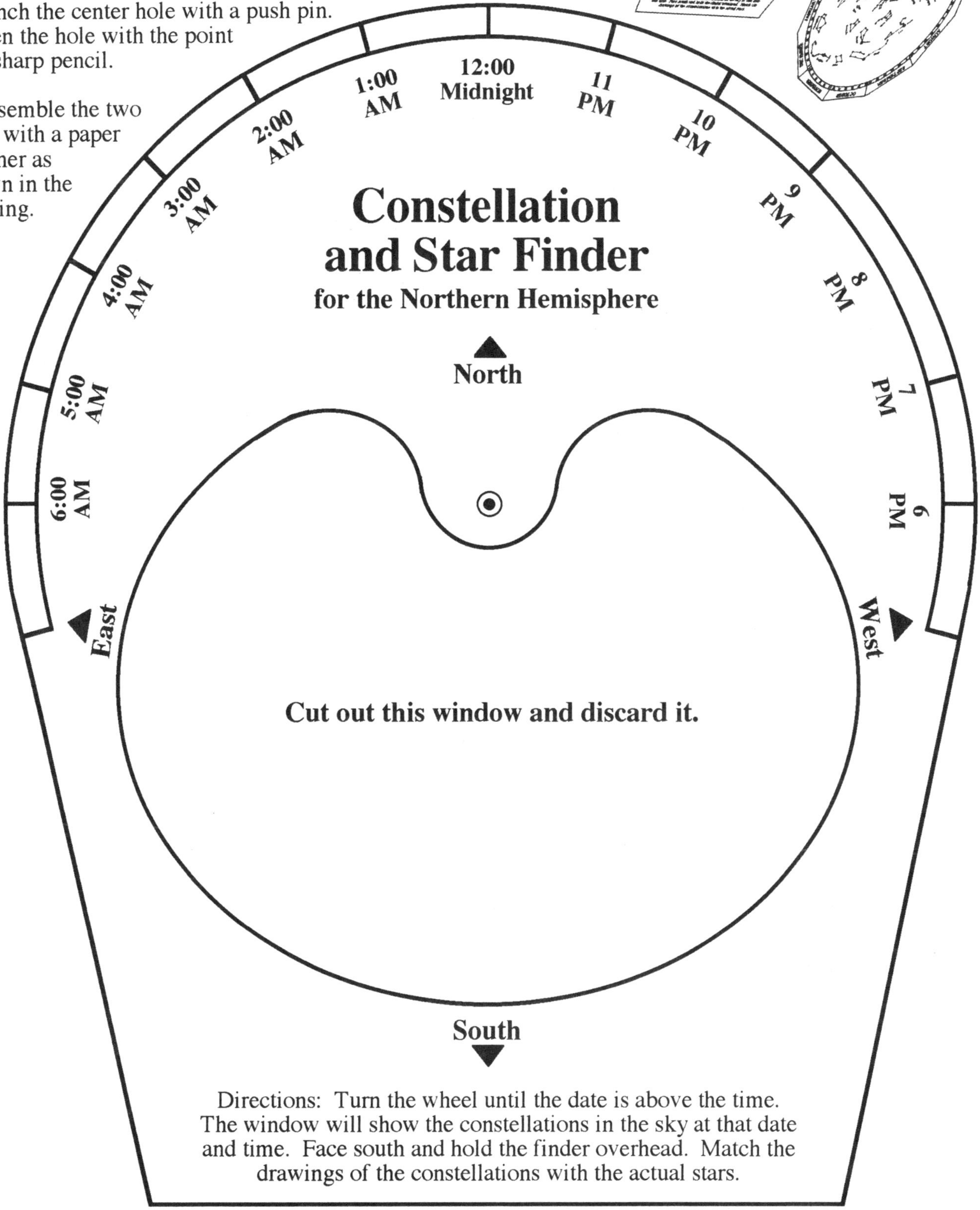

Constellation and Star Finder

Part Two

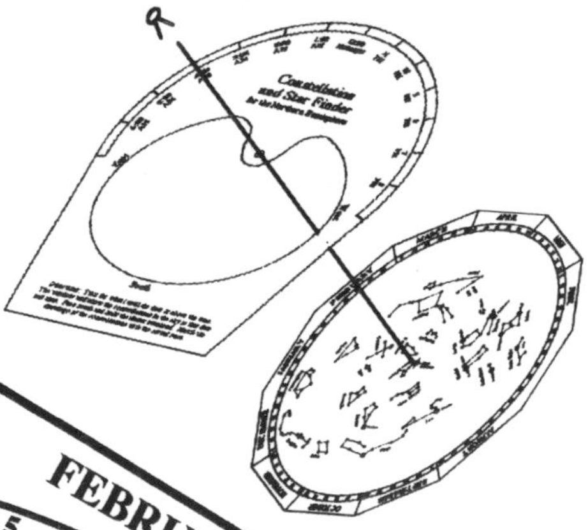

- Glue this page to thin cardstock or half of a file folder. Cut this part of the constellation and star finder out on the solid outside line.
- Punch the center hole with a push pin. Widen the hole with the point of a sharp pencil.
- Assemble the two parts with a paper fastener as shown in the drawing.

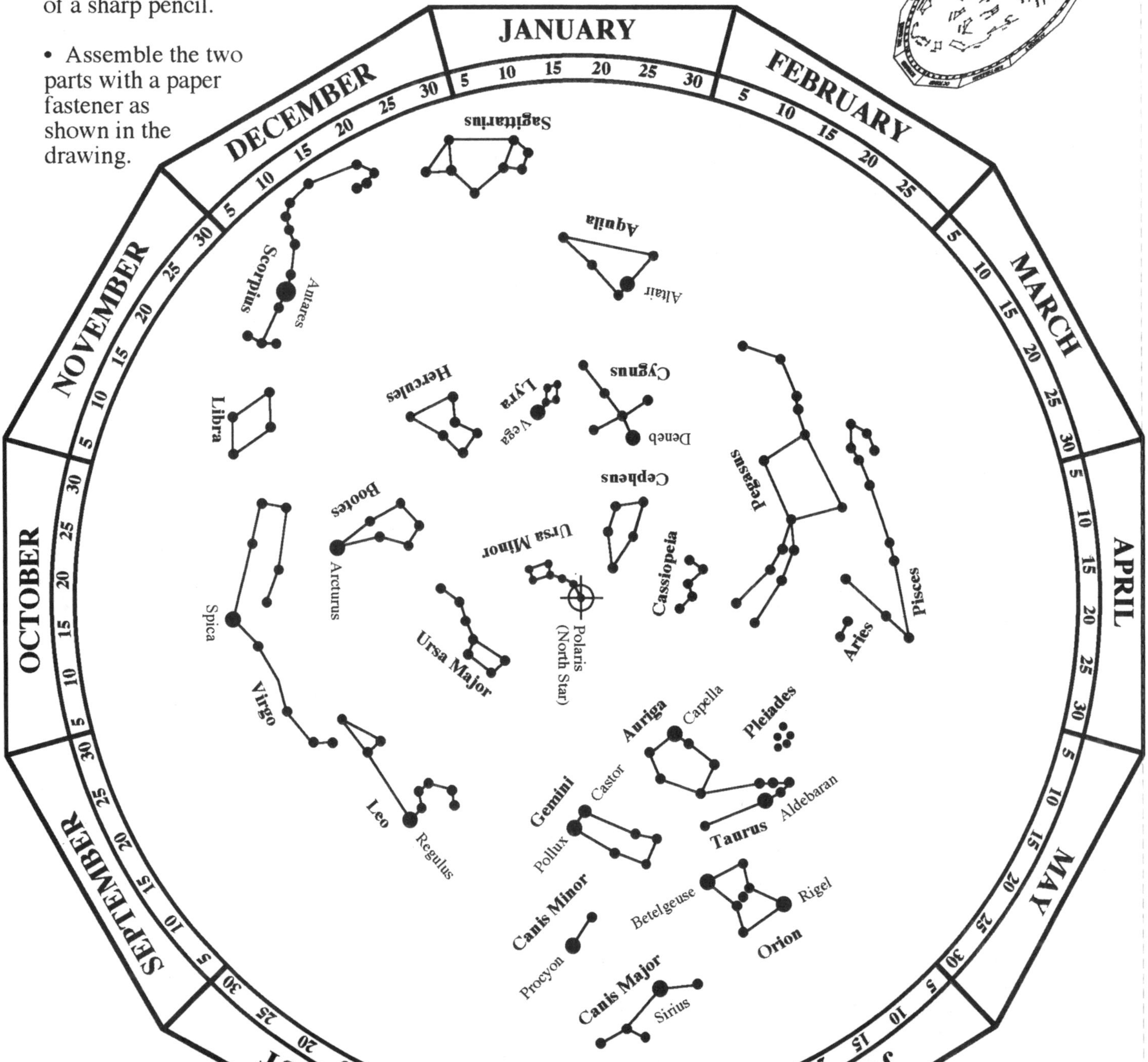

Brainbusters

1. If vowels are worth 25 cents and consonants are worth 5 cents, Which three of these space terms are worth one dollar and twenty-five cents?

Sun, planets, gravity, meteors, comet, binoculars, stars, Mercury, Earth, telescope, asteroids, Jupiter, astronaut, Venus, satellite, constellation

2. The average distance between the Earth and the moon is 400,000 km. The distance between the sun and the Earth is 391 times the distance between the Earth and the moon. At a speed of 300,000 km per second, how long would it take for light to travel from the sun to the Earth?

3. The diameter of Mars is 24.32 kilometers greater than 53% of the diameter of the Earth, which is 12,756 kilometers. What is the diameter of Mars?

4. In this problem, every letter represents one of the numerals from 0 - 9. If you replace the letter with its equivalent numeral, the final answer will be correct. Hints: Every numeral appears at least once. The value of the letter E is zero. The most frequently appearing numeral is one. The least frequently appearing numeral is 2.

```
   VENUS
    MARS
  SATURN
 +URANUS
 -------
 NEPTUNE
```

5. Data: The speed of light is about 300,000 km per second. The Earth is about 40,000 km in circumference. The moon is about ten times the Earth's circumference away from the Earth. Use this information to find out how long it would take a burst of light from Earth to bounce off the moon and return to Earth.

6. One year on Earth is equal to 365.25 days. In its yearly journey around the sun, the Earth covers a distance of 968,000,000 km. Each time you have a birthday, you have ridden the Earth once around the sun. So far, how many kilometers have you traveled?

7. The Earth must travel at a tremendous speed to complete its trip of 968,000,000 km in one year. How far does the Earth travel in the month of June? How far does it travel in a day? (Remember that a year is actually 365.25 days long.) How far does it travel in an hour, a minute, and a second?

8. Tuttle's Comet was discovered in 1790. It reappears every 14 years. Will we see it again this century?

9. The first recorded sighting of what we know as Halley's Comet was made in 294 B.C. It returns every 76 years.

How many times has it appeared since then? When did we last see it? When will we see it again? How old will you be then?

10. If each letter of the alphabet is worth one cent more than the previous letter (A = .01, B = .02, C = .03, etc.), then one of these words is worth exactly one dollar. Which one is it?

Sun, gravity, meteors, Mars, comet, binoculars, stars, Mercury, Earth, telescope, Jupiter, astronaut, planets, Venus, satellite, Uranus

Brainbusters Answers

1. Asteroids, satellite, astronaut

2. There are more zeros in this problem than a calculator can handle. Students will have to either use their knowledge about what to do with zeros in a division problem or be very creative when attacking the problem. It takes light about 8.69 minutes (8 minutes 41 seconds) to travel from the sun to the Earth.

3. According to these calculations, the diameter of Mars is 6,785 km.

4. E=0, N=1, V = 2, S= 3, M = 4, A = 5, U = 6, P = 7, T = 8, R = 9.

VENUS	20,163
MARS	4,593
SATURN	358,691
+URANUS	+695,163
NEPTUNE	1,078,610

5. The moon orbits about 400,000 km away from the Earth. It would take light about 2.67 seconds to make the 800,000 km round trip.

6. Answers will vary depending on the ages of your students and how exact you want to be (year, month, day, hour) when they solve the problem.

7. The Earth travels about 79,500,000 km in June, 2,650,000 km in one day, 110,000 km in one hour, 1,840 km in one minute, and about 30.5 km every second.

8. Yes. Its next appearance will be in the year 2000, which is technically part of the 20th century. The 21st century begins with the year 2001.

9. Input -294 (press 294 then the +/- key on your calculator) and keep adding 76 to it (If you press +,+,76, it makes 76 a constant. Then you only need to keep pressing the equal sign to perform the additions). Halley's Comet has appeared 30 times since it was discoved, 31 if you count its discovery. Its last appearance was in 1986. It should appear again in 2062. Answers to the last question will vary.

10. Telescope = $1.00

Metric Measurement Tools

On this page are the patterns for a Mini Metric Micrometer and a metric tape measure.

- Cut the two portions of this page apart on the dashed line.
- Glue the parts of the Mini Metric Micrometer on this half of the page to cardstock or part of a file folder.

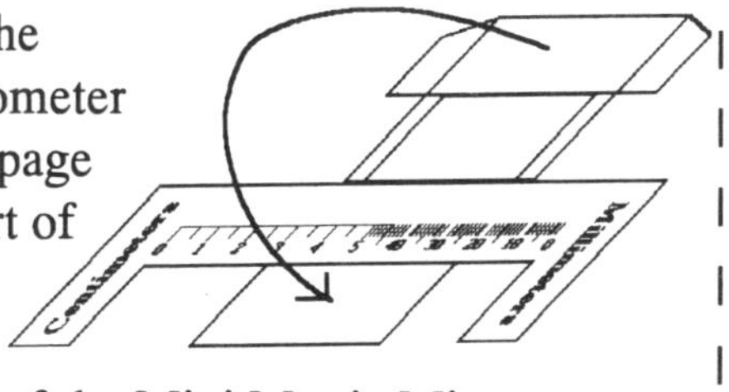

- Cut out both parts of the Mini Metric Micrometer and assemble them according to this drawing and the directions on the back of the micrometer.
- Cut out and assemble the metric tape measure (to keep it flexible, do not glue it to cardstock or a file folder).

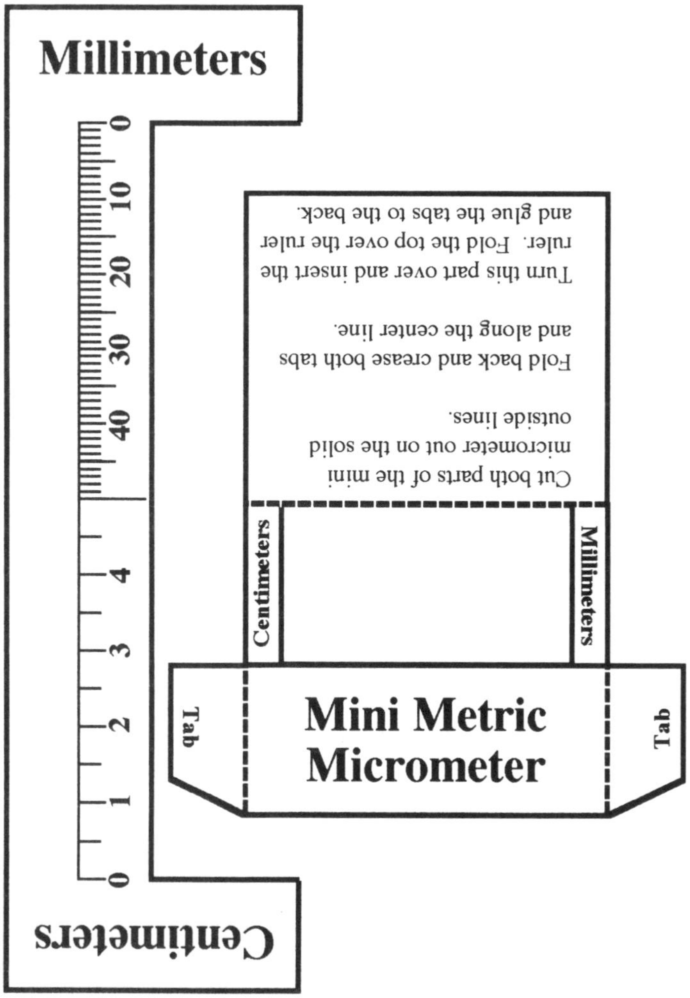

Cut ruler strips apart between the double lines. Glue the strips together to make a one-meter long tape measure.

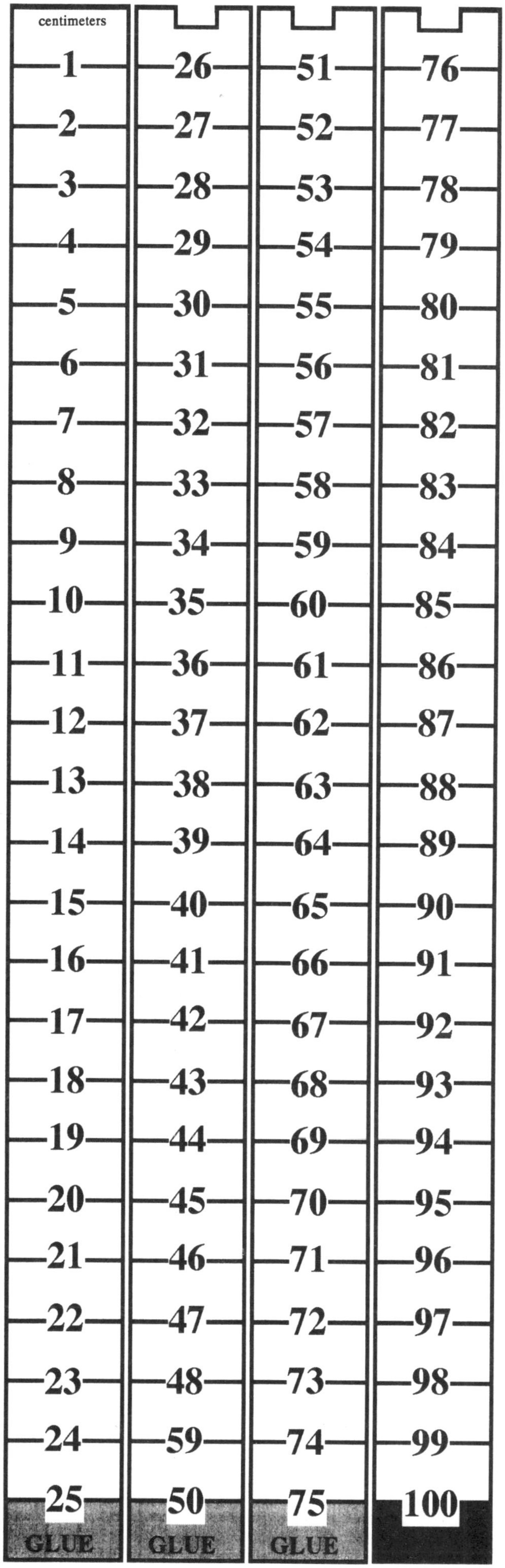

Astrofacts

Date is current April 1994	Distance from Sun in millions of km	Approx. diameter in km	Average temp. in degrees C	Rotation period day, hr, min	Time of one revolution around Sun	Number of moons	Gravity Earth =1	Mass Earth = 1	Density Water = 1	Special Features
Sun	X	1,400,000	10,000	24 d	X	50 +	28	333,000	1.41	Medium sized yellow star
Mercury	58	4,840	430	58d 18h	88 days	0	38	.055	5.42	Probably had liquid water at one time
Venus	103	12,200	500	243d	224.7 days	0	.91	.815	5.25	Sulfuric acid cloud covers planet
Earth	155	12,756	15	23h 56m	365.25 days	1	1	1	5.51	Only planet with liquid water
Mars	228	6,787	-50	24h 37m	687 days	2	.38	.108	3.96	Colored red by iron-rich dust
Jupiter	778	142,200	-150	9h 54m	11.86 years	16	2.6	318	1.33	Giant red spot = 300 Earths
Saturn	1,427	120,600	-18	10h 46m	29.46 years	17	1.1	95.2	.7	So light it would float on water
Uranus	2,870	51,300	-200	17h 12m	84.01 years	5	.9	14.4	1.3	Axis tilted 98 degrees
Neptune	4,497	49,100	-220	16h 30m	164.8 years	8 +	1.2	17.2	1.8	Ninth planet until 1999
Pluto	5,900	2,300	-230	6d 9h	248.5 years	1	.08	.003	2	Geosynchronous orbiting moon

Facts about the Milky Way Galaxy

It is about 100,000 light years (LY) in diameter.
Distance from Earth to the center of galaxy = 30,000 LY
Thickness of the galaxy in the area near Earth = 30,000 LY
Thickness at the edge of the galaxy = 10,000 LY
Rotation speed = 240,000 km per second
One rotation = 230 million years
Nearest neighbor to the Milky Way = Andromeda galaxy
Distance from Earth to the Andromeda galaxy = 2,000,000 LY

Star color	Temp. in °C
Red	4,000
Yellow	6,000
White	9,000
Blue	20,000

Distance from Earth in LY	
Alpha Centauri	4.27
Sirius	8.6
Betelgeuse	520
Polaris	1,086

Facts about light
Light speed 300,000 km per second
One light year = 9,500,000,000,000 km
Radio waves travel at the speed of light

Astronomical Units (AU)
1 AU = one Earth - Sun distance
(approximately 150,000,000 km)